Moving to Costa Rica

Moving to Costa Rica

Expat Essays on Life in Central America

— Hal O'Boyle —

Mira Vacas Publishing
San José, Costa Rica

Published by Mira Vacas Publishing.
San José, Costa Rica
www.The-Extremist.com
www.DemocracyThePaintedWhore.com
www.ABroadInCostaRica.com

Cover Design:
Hal O'Boyle/CreateSpace
Cover Photo:
Sally O'Boyle

ISBN: 9780615387673

Printed in the USA

1 2 3 4 5 6 7 8 9

Introduction & Disclaimer

The essays in this collection appeared between 2006 and 2009 in Key West the Newspaper, a small weekly published by Dr. Dennis Reeves Cooper, in Key West, Florida. The opinions expressed in them are entirely mine and by no means represent those of Dr. Cooper or his publication.

I've found that occasionally people are offended by opinions I express in my essays, or by the manner in which I express them. It is never my intention to offend. I strive for illuminating metaphor, fresh simile, or good natured spoof, and shun overt insult or boorish name calling no matter how richly my subject may deserve it. If I occasionally fall short of my ambitions and offend a thin skinned progressive busybody or officious functionary, I deeply regret it. I apologize to those fragile souls in advance here and now. Everything else being equal, however, I take driving the occasional garden variety world improver into a state of high dudgeon as an indication that the writing has at least some small merit.

Above all I'm concerned that my observations of Costa Rican politics and society might be misconstrued as critical of the people or the country in general. For the record I will say that my experience with Costa Ricans has shown them to be overwhelmingly intelligent, warm, generous, and caring. Their country is no less delightful than the people. If I've taken a few shots at politicians and leftist delusion, it is only because politicians and leftist delusions are the same the world over and make irresistibly easy targets.

I've made every effort to check the information I've relied on in this book. If there are any factual mistakes, they are mine alone. I would urge anyone relying on information found in these essays to check it out on their own before assuming it is true. Their purpose is to inform and entertain and not to render any advice, legal or otherwise, concerning moving to or living in Costa Rica.

Hal O'Boyle
Escazú, Costa Rica
12 July 2010

Contents

Cerbr Health
mp : Covid2021!
RP 12345 abc

A Drive in Never-Never Land

The noise was what I noticed first. Or, I should say, the symphony of noises. I was behind the wheel of a microscopic blue Daihatsu, a rented machine deep into middle age. It had four-wheel drive, five on the floor, and a power plant that looked like an aluminum sewing machine.

I had just pulled out into traffic in San José, Costa Rica. Weeeeeeeeerrrrrrowww went the little engine as I banged it into third at 60 KPH. Chunkachunkachunka-chunka-rattttattattatatt-tatttaatttatatttatata went all the loose parts behind the door panels as we stumbled over a road that appeared to have been paved in shifts by people who were strangers to the task. In the side mirrors, I noticed loose plastic trim fluttering in the wind.

As I sneaked a concerned peek at the loose molding, we hit what I was sure was a land mine. WWHAAAM!!!! The car lurched as the left front wheel disappeared and miraculously re-emerged from a spectacular pothole. My bride in the passenger's seat uttered an astonished prayer, "GAWWWWD," she said.

The locals signaled me and each other in a cheerful tattoo played on their car horns. I thought of my early Boy Scout training in Morse code. No help. There was some sort of communication going on, but I was out of the loop.

Above the background noise, periodic ejaculations issued from the passenger seat. I understood them just fine. "THE DITCH, THE DITCH," she squealed in a choked gasp that reached above the whine of the little engine. She referred not to some unusual geographic feature but to the rain gutter along the side of nearly every road: a concrete culvert two or three feet deep and just as wide. Put a wheel over the edge and you'll have to climb straight up to get out the driver's door.

An oncoming car swerved suddenly across the centerline to avoid a pothole. I swerved toward THE DITCH to avoid him. I'm sure I ran half the tire over the edge. "OH, JESUS," screamed my wife, praying louder now.

That was my moment of epiphany. I was beyond prayer. In my mind I heard myself laughing madly: "HAAAA HAHA HAHA HAHA HAAA-AAAA!" My inner wheelman hollered, "EAT MY DUST, SUCKERS!!!"

I was God's own 14-year-old at the wheel of a smoldering hot bumper car. I was flying through a maze populated by other speed-crazed adolescents. What luck! No one over the age of 16 is allowed to drive in this country. I LOVE this place!

I knew the precise location of the tiny wheels on the road. The screaming engine vibrated a message of total control through the shifter in the palm of my hand. I wore a grin of goofy glee as I topped a rise going waaaay too fast. I slammed down into third gear and dove into the hairpin turn at the bottom of the hill. Weeeeee-rrrroooooowwwwww my sewing machine whined in protest as I shaved the edge of THE DITCH on the inside of the turn.

I wasn't in the mood for whining. The rattling, roaring, banging, and bumping nearly drowned out the flow of urgent advice and terrified screams from the passenger's seat. The roar of blood running hot through my hardening veins deafened me to whatever got through the din.

Pedestrians, bicyclists, buses, trucks and magnificent potholes, potholes like strip mines, were part of the game. I swerved boldly between craters on a section of road that looked like it had suffered a recent mortar attack. I whipped around a bus stopped near the top of a hill. I tapped out a message of life everlasting and glorious redemption on the horn as I crested the blind rise in the wrong lane.

There's our turn! Whip down the tiny back road now to the bridge at the bottom of the hill. THUUUMMP, no pavement on the other side of the bridge. Second gear and up the rutted gravel track . . . steeper . . . steeper . . . shift down to first. The rattling and banging reaches an impossible crescendo while all four wheels shoot gravel and dust back behind us.

There it is, the cobblestone drive of *Finca los Guayabos*, the coffee farm where we are staying. The driveway is so steep I wonder if we will tip over backwards going up. We don't. Stopped in front of our rented *casita*, the silence is deafening. The view over the valley stuns us. We speak in whispers. It's sunny. The temperature is perfect. A cool breeze wafts birdsong and the aroma of flowers over us.

As we get out, admiring the view, a rocket streaks from the valley in front of us. It detonates at eye level. BLAAAM! BLAAAM! Two thunderous blasts rattle the windows. Flocks of birds explode out of the trees.

We notice later that the explosions always come in pairs. It's near Christmas. The locals are celebrating the season. BLAAM! — *FELIZ!* BLAAM! — *NAVIDAD!* Welcome to — BLAAM! BLAAM! — COSTA! RICA!

I can't wait to get back.

Reintroducing the Ends

Much of Costa Rica's appeal for Americans is that living expenses here are supposedly a lot lower than in the U.S. When our income ended after the top of the real estate bubble in 2005, we moved here thinking we'd save a bundle.

While it is true that some things are less expensive, fresh produce or the services of a plumber or gardener, for instance, many things are actually more expensive. Additionally, we live in the suburbs of a big city here, where the cost of living is higher than it is in the countryside.

Rice and beans are cheap, but meat and fish cost about the same here as they do in the U.S. Restaurant dining is about the same as well, and heavily taxed.

Owning a car in Costa Rica is much more expensive than it is in the U.S. Gas is over $4 a gallon. Cars themselves are about double the price of similar models in the U.S. The rough roads batter car suspensions into junk in short order. Drivers spend a lot of time sitting in traffic jams.

There is probably some savings to be had on clothing, if you don't buy imports. And the climate is so uniformly pleasant you don't really need much in the way of clothing.

Housing is cheap if you are content with the Costa Rican standard in housing, which is small and simple. If your taste runs to hot water at every sink, modern electric and plumbing design and granite countertops, housing is comparable in cost to that in typical American cities.

For all of that, however, our family lives here for less than half of what we spent to live in the U.S. And I feel like we live as well.

The explanation, I find, is not that the cost of living here is so much less, it is that we live a much simpler life here. Here we only have one car, no boat, no vacation home, no expensive hobbies. No airplane. Airplane???!!! Yeah, an airplane.

To demonstrate that even normally level headed guys like this writer are not immune to the silliest delusions of never ending prosperity, at the height of the madness, I thought I could afford an airplane. I couldn't, of course. But I had a wonderful time wearing my lampshade hat and dancing on the table. Luckily Hurricane Wilma brought me to my senses by wrecking the plane. I took it as a sign from God and ruefully cashed the insurance check that ended my flying career.

Here in Costa Rica, having practically no income, our family has rediscovered what had for us been a forgotten skill, that of making ends meet. Our ends had been so far apart and for so long, they probably wouldn't have recognized each other if they had met.

We are trying to reacquaint them now. We're conducting the introductions in Spanish in the hope that the relationship will flourish on the charm of a romance language and pure novelty.

It occurs to me that many of you in the Homeland may be considering similar introductions. I recommend this simple formula as a foolproof guide to remaining solvent:

Don't Buy Stuff You Cannot Afford.

The formula for deciding what you can afford is simple, if you must deplete your savings or borrow money to have it, you probably can't afford it. If you can't afford it, go without or substitute something you can afford.

Leave borrowing to pay off current debt to your betters in the U.S. Congress. They will do all the reckless spending they can whether you like it or not. They are, after all, spending your money. You can't live like a government, however, because you only have your own money to spend. Spend it wisely and the ends will continue to meet.

Te Amo Por Siempre

Gabrielle is 11 years old. She's four and a half feet tall and doesn't weigh much more than a couple sacks of groceries. Her black hair shines in the dim light of the dingy classroom as she nervously twirls it in the fingers of her right hand. Her eyes are almost black, the whites bright white; her smile, a contagious flash of fun, bursts like a sunrise from flawless cinnamon skin.

With dogged determination and mixed success she tries to pronounce the word "like" using just one syllable. I suggest she try to use it in a sentence. She gamely asks, "Jew lee-keh choe-koe-lah-teh?" I answer her truthfully, "Yes, I like chocolate." I decide to ignore the confusing complexities of the verb "to do."

She and five other Costa Rican adolescents show up voluntarily to study English three times a week at a little school in Santa Ana, Costa Rica. The school is supported by a private Costa Rican business. This writer volunteers as the *gringo* native speaker. The students are beginners so there is plenty of Spanish spoken, and God knows, this *gringo viejo* needs the practice.

The school is a humble building. There are two single florescent tubes attached crookedly to the ceiling. One of them works, smearing the room with a dim gray light. The floor is bare concrete. The walls show evidence of paint applied long, long ago. Four wires coil down the far wall from two cheap ceiling fans. Five feet above the floor black tape joins them to two other wires protruding from a four-inch hole.

There's a concrete sink in the back of the room and a bookcase with rows of what look to be new, unused books. An old TV mutely occupies the center shelf. A map of Costa Rica hangs on the wall in the space between the single window and the door. Modern white-board covers the front wall.

There are three boys and three girls in the class. Raquella and Maria are a little older than Gabrielle, 14 or 15 maybe. Typically attractive young *ticas*, they wear tight, revealing clothing with plunging necklines. The three boys, Juan, Simón, and Daniél, (the last two pronounced with the accent on the end), all around 14, are more or less constantly distracted by the necklines and the prodding, squealing and giggling of the two older girls. The boys don't seem to mind. Occasional discussion of the English language barely penetrates the swirling hormonal fog.

The Costa Rican teacher speaks excellent English. He teaches eight hours a day in this school.

These are the last two hours of his day. The kids have worn him down and are in full control. Little or no English is spoken. The students are translating a random smattering of English words using English/Spanish dictionaries. Raw beginners, I wonder what use they will make of words like, skull, golf, and proud.

I don't have much to do. The students listen and repeat as I pronounce the words on the board. I answer a few questions. They go back to fooling around and make halting progress in their translation assignment.

Gabrielle comes up to me during a break in class. She tells me she has a girlfriend in the United States. She doesn't know where her girlfriend lives, but thinks it might be in Nueva Jork. She would like to go the United States someday, she says.

We're speaking Spanish. I ask if she goes to school. She says no. I ask why. She says she can't go to school because she is a *nica*. (pronounced neeka) A *nica* is someone from Nicaragua, a minority here, looked down upon by many Costa Ricans. She is an illegal immigrant and doesn't have papers. I think about giving up Spanish so I won't have to discover things like this.

Last week I read an internet report that Costa Rica's child protection agency was threatening to take a child away from an American expat family because, after an intolerably bad experience in a Costa Rican public school, the expats were schooling their eight-year-old son at home. An offended teacher reported them to the Child Protection police.

It turns out that not allowing your child to be bullied by his classmates and ignored by his teacher in a crappy Costa Rican elementary school is the bureaucratic equivalent of "child abuse." Talking to Gabrielle, I was having a disconnect from the mythology of the splendid success of government schooling in Costa Rica. Child Protection bureaucrats were going to force a rich foreign boy to go to a lousy public school while they kept a poor foreign girl from going to any school at all. It occurred to me that public bureaucracies are the same everywhere: self-interested, ineffective, defensive, and vindictive. Education, if it appears at all on a list of priorities, is very close to the bottom.

I didn't know what to say to Gabrielle. I wanted to figure out some way to get her an education. I wanted to take her home and teach her to read myself. But the low trajectory of an uneducated life didn't concern her. She was much more interested in the romantic poetry of Latin pop music. She wanted to know how it sounded in English.

"What is the English for *Eres bonita*?" she asked.

I answer, "You are beautiful." Beautiful is a challenging mouthful of vowels for the native speaker of Spanish. She repeated it many times. "You are beautiful. You are beautiful. You are beautiful." She loved saying it. After a dozen tries she was understandable, sounding like a pixie *bandida* in a spaghetti western.

She also wanted to know the English for that timeless touchstone of Latin crooning, *"Te amo por siempre."* "How do you say it?" she asked, delightfully unselfconscious, as if *"Te amo por siempre"* were the name of a bus stop.

"I love you forever," I answered. She made me repeat it a dozen times, imitating me after each one until she thought she had it just about right. Then she ran over and tried it out on Daniel. He seemed pleased.

Security Esthetics

When we moved to Costa Rica a year and a half ago, the prison like façades that faced the streets of San José appalled us. Steel security bars and razor tape are everywhere. We were delighted that our first house was safe enough in the middle of a large coffee plantation that it needed neither bars nor wire. The five big, not-that-friendly dogs and attentive longtime employees provided reliable security.

A move across the valley to a suburb closer to the city gave us a new perspective on security. With a small, underpaid police force and equally small consequences for getting caught thieving, the locals believe in prevention.

Our house is surrounded by an 8-foot brick wall. On top of the wall is a four-foot iron fence. We have a monitored alarm with door and window triggers and motion detectors. The doors are double bolted and have iron gates in front of them. Bars cover every window. The electric garage door is padlocked at night. There are three ferocious looking, but otherwise useless dogs living in the yard.

We feel pretty safe here. Despite the landlady's sincere warning against never leaving the house empty, sometimes we have no choice.

"They're watching you," she said. I didn't believe her.

"They will steal the light fixtures and the toilets," she said. Once again I was incredulous. Is there really a black market in hot toilets? We're talking low value density here. But what do I know about it?

The house has an impressive view of the valley. When we first arrived we were glad there was no razor wire atop the fence to mar the view and complete the prison yard chic that begins with the walls and bars.

It's funny how the simplest incident can change your notion of what looks good.

My wife and the boys were traveling. I was in the house alone for a week. Now and then I had to leave it empty. On one of those occasions someone tried to break in. The landlady was right, they are watching. Chico didn't make it into the house, just the yard. Apparently I scared him away without seeing him. He dropped his baseball cap in the mud, a red and black number with a Chevrolet logo on it. He left footprints on the wall next to the bars he was trying to bend apart. He had to have climbed the wall at one of the low spots. I decided to make that a lot harder.

Even if he had been successful at getting in the house, I thought comfortingly, he would never get the toilet out through the bars. He would have set off the motion detector alarms. The alarm guys would have been here in 10 minutes.

No matter. I was going to defend my space, if not my toilet. Suddenly, razor tape didn't look so ugly.

Its predecessors have had many names, barbed wire, thorn wire, and the devil's rope among them. Inventor Joe Glidden came up with a workable model in 1874. He won the patent battle in 1887. Soon after, in San Antonio, Texas, Bet-A-Million Gates showed how effective it was in containing wild cattle. Bet-A-Million's marketing skills and promotional ability triumphed over the open range opposition, and he made a fortune. Attitudes toward barbed wire had to be changed then, too, just like mine was here in Central America. Some blood flowed in the Fence Cutter Wars, but attitudes did indeed change.

Barbed wire ended the era of open range grazing in the Old West and changed the face of the land forever. Before the end of the 19th century it had become not only an agricultural tool but a weapon. It was the weapon I needed.

The French introduced barbed wire as a military obstacle in the 1880s. By the end of WWI in 1918, entanglements of barbed wire had become famous death traps for many a hapless soldier. Barbed wire and its more modern offspring, razor tape and concertina wire, are now used throughout the world wherever there is a need to control meat with metal.

Control meat with metal was exactly what I wanted to do. It's funny how footprints on the wall next to my desk so quickly extinguished any aesthetic objections I had to coils of razor wire.

We had three choices, electric wire, razor tape or concertina wire. Concertina takes its name from the accordion like musical instrument. Coils of concertina wire form a double helix and open like the bellows of that instrument. It is the most effective obstacle, but costs almost three times as much as the simpler razor tape. Electric fence costs a little less than concertina but needs maintenance. We went with the least expensive, maintenance free choice, stainless steel razor tape.

Within a week it was installed. Two bucks a foot, which was more than the value of all the toilets in the house, but less than one laptop. It now twinkles cheerfully atop the four foot iron fence that itself stands atop the brick wall. I'm trying to remember what I thought was so ugly about it.

Keeping the Vice Squad Private

R oman Catholicism is the official government religion here in Costa Rica, although *ticos* don't seem to care what *your* religion is. Having an official religion appears to provide Costa Ricans a sensible and wonderfully tolerant attitude toward sin. Perhaps it's the convenience of the Sacrament of Penance. Or maybe it's the cultural effect of the graceful Spanish word for sin, *pecado*. A *pecado* sounds like such a charmingly trivial item, something for which one would never condemn a *caballero* (gentleman) . . . or his *doña*, (lady), for that matter.

Official government sin policy is sensible, tolerant and understanding of human weakness. All the most common vices, drinking, gambling, and prostitution are legal here. It is by no means an endorsement or, even less, a recommendation. Costa Ricans are aware of the ruinous social pathology that springs from overindulgence in any of them. They are also smart enough to realize that criminalizing sin won't make it go away. It will simply turn sinners into criminals.

A recent newspaper article discussed an American hotel owner's campaign to stamp out prostitution in his hotel. There's a one man vice squad, thought I, bringing the benefits of American prudery and moral superiority to the benighted peasants of Central America. Of course, a private property owner has the right to do as he pleases with his property. If the self-righteous owner is set on checking every couple who enters his hotel to somehow determine what they are going to do in their private room and whether any money will change hands as a result, more power to him.

What struck me, however, was the owner's complaint as to how much money his policy had cost him. Thousands, he complained. It seems to me, if he wants to puff out his chest with the courage of his moral convictions, risk insulting fathers with their daughters, and guests who favor heavy make-up, he might have the dignity not to whine about the cost.

That incident, and other related public discussions of "sex tourism," is evidence of *gringo* moral prudery creeping into Costa Rican affairs. It is estimated that up to 10% of Costa Rica's visitors are here as "sex tourists." How they determine this figure is unclear, but the statistic is tossed about as if it were Holy Writ. No one ever considers that it's only because the geezers have to risk jail time to buy a piece in their own country that they come here at all. I think it was George Carlin who asked, "If sex is legal and selling is legal, why isn't selling sex legal?"

What we are talking about here is erotic commerce between consenting adults, not the sale of children to the degenerate or sex slavery. As it should be, the crime of having sex with children or with anyone not a willing participant is punished here by long stays in really nasty prisons. But pressure by the morally superior to interfere with the private affairs of willing adults persists even in the face of Costa Rica's common sense policies toward vice.

Criminalizing vice has never done much to eliminate it. For proof one need look no further than America's experiment with alcohol prohibition, and its ongoing failures to prevent gambling, prostitution, and drug abuse. If anything, banning vice has done more harm than good, corrupting not only the sinners but ultimately those charged with keeping sinners from their private sins.

Organized crime in the U.S. got a running start during alcohol prohibition in the twenties. Vice squads everywhere are notoriously corrupt outfits that end up skimming the profits of vice rather than suppressing it. And the War on Drugs has become one of the largest money making government enterprises in history. It has spread the uniquely American myth that sin can be ended by banning it to nearly every country in the world.

Uncle Sam is generously providing the locals with all the high tech gear of the Drug War in hopes of dragging them ever more enthusiastically into the highly lucrative and totally futile effort to stamp out drug use. Costa Ricans have not yet hit upon the War on Drugs as a money making enterprise. By U.S. standards, *ticos* are real slackers when it comes to kicking in doors and confiscating property. *Gracias a dios.*

We can only hope that *tico* common sense will manage to resist American efforts to escalate the Drug War and that the attempt to identify and frustrate sinners in San José will remain limited to private vice squads in selected hotels.

Selling the Sizzle

Asset bubbles are the result of easy credit and a natural human desire to get something for nothing. The long-term increase in all prices and the occasional price explosion for certain assets occurs primarily because there is no standard for the unit we use to measure value. The dollar is an article of faith, undefined, as ethereal as fairy dust. Tinkerbelle, like the dollar, flies only if we believe she can.

The dollar represents no fixed amount of a hard-to-find commodity, like gold or silver. The value of every existing dollar is constantly diluted as more dollars are created to fund government deficits and consumer desires. It is impossible to accurately compare prices from one year to the next without reference to highly suspect statistics produced by the very outfit that benefits most from the dilution, the U.S. government.

It is true there were booms and busts in the 19th century when an international gold standard kept government deficits and reckless consumer spending tightly reined. They were, however, local phenomena, fueled by local credit expansion and speculative dreams. They were torrid flings, rather than life-long affairs. And, like love affairs, the beginnings were always more pleasant than the ends. Recovery was generally swift, the damage not life threatening.

The first of what would become much larger and more destructive bubbles occurred in the 20s, shortly after the Federal Reserve took control of the dollar. The Florida real estate boom of the mid 1920s, the stock market boom that ended in 1929 and the subsequent depression in the 1930s were products of currency manipulation by the Fed.

Franklin Roosevelt kept the game going by confiscating America's gold at $20 an ounce, denying Americans refuge from his plans for a better world. He then promptly revalued gold to $35, adding insult to injury.

But it wasn't until 1971 that the dancer's last balloon hit the hot end of the cigar. That's when President Nixon, realizing the U.S. was bankrupt, cut the dollar loose from gold entirely. The world at that point had a choice, admit their biggest customer was busted and go down with him, or keep pretending dollars were as good as gold. They opted for fantasy.

Since then the bubbles have become larger and their bursting more destructive. As the discipline of honest money left the marketplace, so too have the habits of character that make for prosperity in an honest marketplace. Hard work, innovation, and thrift have been driven from the field by speculation, easy money, and greed. Why sweat and toil in some dreary occupation, consumed with stress and drudgery when you can become rich beyond dreams of avarice by simply buying things and selling them a little later to someone not quite as smart as you?

The problem is that no real wealth is created by inflationary schemes. As asset value rises on one side of the balance sheet, debt rises on the other. The game is challenging and fun as individuals try to jigger their personal balance sheets and get out of the game before the jiggering comes to a stop. "Musical chairs" comes to mind.

When the dollar came untethered from gold, the stage was set for the first global credit and money expansion. A recent visit to the Pacific coast of Costa Rica, where a major land boom is in full cry, shows that few places, no matter how remote, will escape being swept up in the frenzy that easy money creates.

Costa Rica's Pacific coast between Ojochal and Dominical is now referred to locally as "The Gold Coast." Dirt has surely turned to gold for those lucky enough to have bought land there before 2005. Though probably fewer than 2,000 souls live in the area, the finest highway in the country runs along the coast there. Less than five years old, it's a modern marvel of roadway engineering:

wide, smooth, and, these days, travelled almost exclusively by real estate speculators.

From Dominical to Ojochal, stunning, jungle-covered mountains descend to a warm, clear sea. In the hills facing the ocean, swarms of bulldozers and back hoes carve new roads and building sites into the red dirt under the jungle. On land that was never terribly productive for raising cattle, developers have discovered its real value: an ocean view, often panoramic.

Land that Costa Rican farmers sold for what appeared to them to be all the money in the world, has been subdivided, equipped with roads, water, and electricity, and is now being resold. It turns out there is a great deal more money in the world. Enough to raise the price of quarter acre lots to between $100,000 and $200,000. Larger lots cost far more.

There is no doubt that it is indeed beautiful land and they aren't making any more of it. Everyone believes rich people will arrive by the thousands as soon as there is an airport and hospital. Everyone is predicting 30% per year increases in land values until the end of time. Maybe both will happen.

Money fleeing the fast draining punch bowls of the North American and European real estate fiestas has found a new party in full swing here in tiny Costa Rica. "The Gold Coast" is an all real estate economy now. Everyone is in the business or selling land of their own. The similarities to the atmosphere in 2005 Florida are unsettling to one who was there. But, for now, the market is as hot as a grill ready for the steaks, and the sizzle is for sale.

Reporting the Balecera

Though Costa Rica is often called the Switzerland of Central America, there are precious few similarities in the defense strategies of the rifle-bearing Swiss and the demilitarized *ticos*.

Costa Rica's two-time former president, Nobel Peace Prize winner Oscar Arias, is proud there are no arms factories in his country and that Costa Rica would be as helpless as a puppy if attacked by any military force. He is a firm believer in safety through cheerful defenselessness. He has rarely passed up an opportunity to cut a gun in half in public and extol the virtues of civilian disarmament.

Costa Rica famously has no military, relying instead, without any formal treaty, on the goodwill of the United States for its protection against sometimes hostile neighbors. The policy has worked surprisingly well. Costa Rica avoided the horrific slaughter of the Central American civil wars of the 70s and 80s, enjoyed abundant American investment and is now arguably the most prosperous and peaceful country in the region.

In their private lives, however, Costa Ricans are more sanguine about the usefulness of firearms in preserving the peace. There is a firm faith in an ounce of prevention. Armed guards are everywhere. In front of banks, grocery stores, furniture stores, car dealerships, or any establishment where any appreciable amount of cash may change hands, you find men wearing body armor and carrying guns.

Costa Ricans may legally own and carry guns for their own protection, though it is getting harder every year. The rules are similar to those for concealed carry in most U.S. jurisdictions, except the guns have to be registered along with those who carry them.

Gun permit holders have to take a psychological and a marksmanship test. I have no idea what the psych test is like. But I've heard you have to take the shooting test with the shot-out old iron at the testing center. You can't use your own gun because, with seamless bureaucratic logic, before you pass the test you are not allowed to carry your own gun outside your home. If you can hit anything smaller than a beer truck with the antiques at the testing center, you are a good shot indeed.

No shooting test is necessary, by the way, for a shotgun, the most popular weapon among bank and armored truck guards. I guess the reasoning is that accuracy is less critical with sufficient fire-power.

As soon as my Spanish was good enough to read a newspaper, I noticed that when a good guy shoots a bad guy here, it gets just as much ink as when it happens the other way around.

Maybe it's the language. Spanish has a way of softening hard, tough Anglo-Saxon. In Spanish a shootout is a *balacera*. It sounds like something featuring finger sandwiches, chiffon-draped debutantes, and waltz music. Maybe they report all the *balaceras* because they are so rare and sound like such fun events.

A recent story in *La Nacion*, the biggest San José daily, reported that a gunman shot a knife-wielding mugger dead as the mugger threatened to stab a female tourist at a bus stop. The shooter didn't hang around to talk to police. Witnesses were hazy about what he looked like.

But everybody seemed impressed with his shooting ability: one to the chest, one to the head. The bad guy departed this world before his knife hit the ground. "*Tirador experto* (expert shooter)," said *La Nacion*. Can't argue with that. Nobody seemed too concerned about finding the shooter, least of all the police.

Just two days ago there was a report of a messenger who was confronted by two revolver-bearing thugs. The messenger pulled out his 9mm pistol and shot them both. One died a day later. The other is in the hospital under arrest. No charges were brought against the messenger. The police checked to see if he had a permit and that his gun was registered. He did and it was. They gave the piece back to him and said *buen dia* (good day). For all you could tell from the story, they might have said *buen trabajo*, good job.

In the U.S., the messenger would never have been allowed to go home with his gun, or to go home at all for that matter. No matter what happened he would need a good lawyer. Even if he wasn't charged, he would need legal help for protection from the lawsuit the wounded thug would file against him.

And would a story like this have made the papers in the U.S.? Not likely. When civilians use guns to defeat thugs in the U.S., the media doesn't think it is worth reporting.

Consider the shooting that was halted by two armed students at the Appalachian School of Law in Grundy, VA in 2002. A Lexis-Nexis search two weeks after the event, reported by James Eaves-Johnson in The Daily Iowan, showed that of 88 stories about it, only two reported that the students who stopped the shooter were armed.

A similar Lexis-Nexis search on the school shooting in Pearl, Mississippi found 687 articles written about it. Only 19 reported that Assistant Principal Joel Merick had gotten his gun from his car and held the shooter at gunpoint for almost five minutes before police arrived.

The numbers weren't much different on reports of the Edinboro, Pennsylvania restaurant owner who held a student shooter at gunpoint for over 11 minutes until police arrived.

Media bias? What media bias?

But it is the overwhelming media bias against guns that helps lead Americans to think there is safety in helplessness and only bad guys use guns.

I would never have thought I would have to move to a tiny, demilitarized, socialist country in Central America to get honest reporting on private citizens using guns for self-defense.

Perhaps a little Spanish charm and poetry would help with the truth. If we start calling shootouts *balaceras*, perhaps people who use guns to protect the innocent and keep the peace will get as much ink and air time as thugs and gangsters.

An Easter People

The citizens of Costa Rica celebrated the defining event of their spiritual lives yesterday, Easter Sunday. I was pleased and privileged to join them.

A week of warm up called *Semana Santa*, Holy Week, brings in the holiday with processions, rites and rituals. Easter is one of few holidays not celebrated here with rolling barrages of fireworks. Drums, not explosions, mark the tempo of *Pascua*.

The rhythm is a slow, steady tump . . . tump . . . tump . . . tattatattatta . . . tump . . . tump . . . tump. The larger processions include some brass, saxophones, a glockenspiel or two. Crowds chant the rosary in Spanish while they follow a life-sized image of the suffering Jesus carried on the shoulders of a dozen or more men. Homes along the route sport flowers, ribbons, balloons and an occasional impromptu shrine. The week of preparation culminates in the celebration of *La Resurrección*.

The resurrection of Jesus Christ's battered, two-day-dead body is what establishes Christianity's unique selling position. It's the event that Christians believe lifts Christ's claim to revealed truth above that of other, equally popular moral teachers. If religion is about dealing with the mystery of death, Christ's conquest of death clearly defines brand superiority.

The other great teachers had none of Christ's nepotistic claims to inside contacts, and certainly didn't rise from the dead. They didn't claim exclusivity like Christ does in John 14:6, "I am the way and the truth and the life. No one comes to the Father except through me."

The claim of exclusivity annoys many, but, exclusive or not, the key ingredient of Christian salvation is faith in the resurrection and the hope it gives mankind.

If it never happened, Christ is a nobody, regardless of his qualities as a moral teacher. If he didn't get up out of his tomb, Christianity is a fraud. In Christian theology, it is the resurrection of the flesh that redeems the spirit; the return to life makes everything new and gives all important hope to the living. Hope drives all that's best in the human enterprise.

Famous Christians like St. Paul agree, " . . . if Christ has not been raised, our preaching is useless and so is your faith." (I Cor. 14:15) Saint Augustine described Christians as well as they can be described, "We are an Easter people, and Hallelujah is our song."

On Easter morning, I was an unbeliever among the faithful wandering *Parque Central* in San José. A popular haven for preachers, I had never seen it so busy. A semi-pro in a brown and white monk's robe held a white, rubber tipped staff. He preached in the northwest corner, in loud, sonorous Spanish.

The amateurs at my favorite spot in the shade fifty yards away practically had to take numbers. There were at least four: a woman in a yellow flowered blouse, a man with a Bible and a toolbox, a man dressed in an electric blue jumpsuit, and a short guy with a guitar. They took turns declaring the glory of *Jesús Cristo* to a spotty crowd. They seemed to have an agreement about how long each would speak and in what order.

In the Cathedral at the end of the park, Masses were being said end to end. The building is enormous, big as, well . . . big as a cathedral. Spectacular stained glass windows washed the congregation in a soft gold light. There were hundreds of people in the church, coming and going at random. Kids played in the side aisles. The priest had a strong voice and a powerful PA system. His bald head gleamed in the gold light. His gold vestments matched the light perfectly.

I arrived as candles were set on the altar for a High Mass. The warm up praying, preaching, and singing was steady. I was surprised to recognize familiar folk tunes. They sang "When the Saints Go Marching In," without the New Orleans bounce and with strange Spanish lyrics. There was no Miguel in "Michael, Row the Boat Ashore." "Rock of Ages" seemed oddly out of place in a Catholic church. Between songs there was a lot of talk of *vida, sangre, cuerpo y alma*. Life, blood, body and soul. Spanish has the mysterious appeal of the Latin rituals from my childhood.

Praying and singing moved seamlessly into the Mass. The priest chanted his lines in a high, clear tenor in the Gregorian style. The congregation replied in kind. The sound echoed dreamily in the vaulted stone.

There were no hymnals. Enough people knew the responses to carry the timid along. Tears were wiped from a few eyes at the Mass' climax when wine and bread became blood and flesh.

The priest sang, one by one, the revealed truths of Christianity. After each a thousand voices sang a seven note reply, *"Cray-ay-o, yo Cray-ay-o!"* I believe, I do believe!

A little later, St. Thomas' Easter people sang their song. They sang a sweet, soft Hallelujah in reply to the priest's chant. Each time they replied, they sang it three times—three soft, four-note hallelujahs, the second and third slight variations of the first. Everyone knew the notes. They sang a full, delicious chord. They made a peaceful, buoyant, joyous sound. It flooded the enormous room as only a thousand hopeful voices can.

I lamented the cynical lack of faith that kept me apart from the Easter people, but was glad they graciously pretended not to notice. I left before the end of the Mass feeling strangely hopeful, quietly humming their song.

The Crawling Peg

The Crawling Peg sounds like a rock group that isn't too proud to beg for a gig, or that gets so lubed up during one that dancing is impossible except on all fours. It's nothing so cheerful, however.

Here in Costa Rica, "the crawling peg" refers to the narrow spread of buy and sell prices for the local currency, the *colón*. Costa Rica's central bankers refer to it as a system of "controlled devaluation." That's because the value of the *colón* only moves one way—down—against anything of fixed value. Particularly good measures of its value are those things that are hard to create more of, like land, gasoline, chicken, and gold.

The Crawling Peg is much in the news recently because the central bank has decided to allow the *colón* to move within a wider range of prices against the dollar. This has created a lot of uncertainty about the future value (in dollars) of the local money. People living here are used to their currency deteriorating at an alarming but relatively predictable rate. The new rules make the immediate future value of the *colón* more uncertain, but its ultimate value of zero, like that of the dollar, has never been in doubt.

Since Costa Rica's most recent bankruptcy in the mid 80s, the *colón* has gone from a little under 10 to the dollar to a little over 500. And keep in mind that the dollar itself is hardly a fixed benchmark. In that same time, the value of a dollar fell by about half, unless you want to buy a house in Florida, in which case it just plain crashed.

I'm a great admirer of the pious, official, bald-faced lie. That's why I love listening to central bankers talk about what they are doing to control inflation. They talk about inflation as if it were an unstoppable natural phenomenon, like earthquakes or hurricanes. In reality, inflation is no more natural than the local grocer short-weighing your order. A central banker explaining inflation is like a kleptomaniac explaining why removing alarms and firing security guards will help him deal with his problem.

Central banks don't fight inflation, they produce it. They print money for the government to cover the difference between tax collections and the cost of supporting an enormous political class of paper pushers, enforcers, and pensioners. Inflation is a mechanism for stealing money from people who work and giving it to people who vote.

Central bankers are the guys in expensive suits and cushy offices who are well paid to broker the scam and hide the evidence. Here in Costa Rica, they exchanged exploitation of the poor by a few land owners to exploitation of the poor by a large political class of government beneficiaries. Central bankers run the whole sorry con.

So naturally, when the suits decide to change the way they calculate the take from their swindle, some of us become suspicious that the scheme might somehow cost us more than it does now. Clearly, the new plan has nothing to do with controlling inflation. Inflation could be stopped immediately by simply not printing up money for the government whenever it runs short.

Changing the exchange rules doesn't effect inflation at all, but can capture temporary relative advantage against other currencies. In this country, as in most countries in the world, there is only one other currency worth talking about, the U.S. dollar. By any measure, Uncle Sam has been printing up new dollars at a breathtaking pace. Maintaining the global empire isn't cheap and American taxpayers are in no position to pay cash.

Borrowing from our enemies and the Fed is the only way to fight terror and spread freedom. Borrowing dollars into existence works the same for the U.S. as it does for banana republics everywhere. Each new dollar means every old one is worth less. Perhaps the suits here in Costa Rica have seen an opportunity to take advantage of the deteriorating condition of the dollar. Early results, to the great surprise of the clueless, show the *colón* strengthening against the dollar.

Jiggering the exchange rules won't do more than temporarily affect the relative winners and losers in the game. It certainly won't do anything to "control inflation" or strengthen or weaken the local tokens, except as they are valued against other paper tokens.

In a world where there is only unbacked paper money, we can picture national currencies like skydivers without parachutes vying for position as they fall through the air, each hoping to be the last to hit the ground.

As Voltaire said, "All paper money eventually returns to its intrinsic value." Monkeying with the exchange rules is just twisting and turning as you fall through the air. It may delay the inevitable, but it won't repeal the law of gravity or make a golden parachute less valuable.

Geezers with Guns

They hoped to scare me, but comforted me instead. The half inch high headline in *La Nacion*, one of Costa Rica's leading daily newspapers, shouted in alarm:

"Over 20% of *Tico* Police Over 50 Years Old".

In the subhead we learned that most cops 'suffer stress and pains of the feet and column vertebral.' I've got news for *La Nacion*, such suffering is not unique to aging gumshoes.

And somehow the venerable age of the force doesn't bother me. My inner geezer loves the idea that cooler, more experienced officials are more numerous among lawmen here than you might expect in such a young country.

The editors of *La Nacion* were obviously distressed by the number of *ancianos* or geezers, on the force. They were deeply concerned that fleet-footed, youthful members of the *hampa*, as the criminal underclass is known, would dance rings around elderly pursuers.

Characteristically, the papers refer to the *hampa* as though it were a trade union. The country is so deeply invested in carving up markets for special interests that you might expect card-carrying pickpockets and second story men to picket local police stations to keep elderly cops on the job. They probably won't have to. Costa Rican labor laws are such that private employees essentially own their jobs.

Public employees? Forget about it. It would be easier to uproot oaks than remove aging policemen from the force. And probably just as bad an idea.

The age profile of the Costa Rican police force is more in line with the population of more developed countries. Where the median age of the country as a whole is a youthful twenty-something, that of richer countries, like the U.S., is closer to the age of men in their prime: mid-thirties or so. It could be argued that judicious law enforcement is better served by the maturity and sound judgment of an older force.

As to the question of chasing down the swift and strong members of the *hampa*, who cares? It doesn't happen often. And even if a cop caught a running thief, petty theft is hardly punished at all here. It's hardly worth the effort. If the crook is really violent or nasty, all the geezers have guns. Even the appallingly decrepit preserve the ability to squeeze a trigger long past the years when they were running their best times in the 100 yard dash.

The article's author interviewed cops as old as 68. All were healthy and fit foot patrolmen. Most cops here walk rather than ride and doughnut shops are rare. All the interviewees said they felt fine, liked their work, and enjoyed serving their country and their community. I believe them.

And there are ways to keep old cops the equal of young crooks. Cops here carry a wild variety of weapons. You see everything from battered .22 target pistols to Uzi's in police holsters. My son had a few suggestions for special weapons for aging cops that would overcome any age related disadvantages.

The beanbag shotgun was at the top of his list for equipping doddering lawmen. Sprinting pick-pockets would hear, "Outrun this, Chico!" in Spanish right before being bowled over from behind by a couple of hurtling beanbags.

His second idea was a special shotgun round modeled after the traditional throwing weapon of the Argentine gaucho, the *Tres Marías*, or *boleadora*. The round would feature three soft, heavy projectiles connected by strong cord. Aimed at the feet of a fleeing target, it would have no trouble tripping up the swiftest bad guy. The gauchos use such weapons to bring down animals as large as cattle.

The advantages of a mature, experienced force are worth the technological investment. I like to think that experience, cunning and technology are more than enough to allow the aging forces of good to prevail over youthful bad guys. Overcoming the disadvantages of Costa Rica's older cops is as simple as equipping the right geezer with the right gun.

Acts of Faith

T he day breaks on August 2 here in San José, Costa Rica with brass bands blaring and fireworks booming. The pilgrims who have filled the roads for the last few weeks have mostly arrived by now in Cartago, a city about 15 miles east of San José.

Cartago has three times been destroyed by the volcano that looms above it and three times rebuilt, most recently with one of the finest churches in the land. Each year, pilgrims come by the thousands from all over the country, walking, riding horses or motor scooters, even running marathon-style.

They come to honor the country's patron saint, *la Negrita*, the little black girl, the *Virgen de los Angeles*. The holiday stems from a legend of a miracle that began on August 2, 1635.

A woman collecting firewood found a small dark stone standing atop a larger stone in the woods. Looking closer, she saw that the small stone was carved with an image of the Virgin Mary with Baby Jesus in her arms. The woman took the image home and put it in a basket.

The next day she returned to the same place and found a carved image of a snake on the same stone in the same place. She brought that one home too. She went to put it in the same basket as the first image, but the first one was gone. She locked the remaining image up so that no one could take it.

She returned a third time to the place in the woods and found the image of the Virgin Mary on the same stone again. She took it back home only to find that now the snake was gone.

At this point, the town priest was brought in for a consultation. He took charge of the image but nothing changed. The image continued to disappear and reappear where it had been found. After the stone was placed in a locked box in the church and, once again, mysteriously returned to its perch in the woods, the townspeople surrendered. A basilica was built to house the miraculous image where it was so determined to be.

Inside the basilica is a shrine to *la Negrita* where the stone is displayed on its own altar. The chamber is festooned with trinkets and small gifts, many small gold or metallic images of body parts cured through the intervention of the sacred stone.

Many pilgrims climb the church steps on their knees, giving thanks for favors granted or praying for favors to come. Visitors also pray by the stone on which *la Negrita* was originally found and collect water from the stream near the shrine, which is said to have curative powers.

The Costa Rican government declared *la Negrita* the Patron Saint of Costa Rica on September 23, 1824. In 2003, the official count of pilgrims to Cartago was over 1.5 million. That's over 40% of the population of the entire country, and well over half the adults. Such a celebration and display of faith has no North American equivalent.

Costa Ricans are tolerant of other religions, but, according to the 1949 Constitution, Catholicism is the official state religion. The Catholic religion is taught in the public schools and over three quarters of the population considers itself Catholic. Although only 40% admit to active practice, more than that show up every year in Cartago to make sure *la Negrita* hasn't disappeared again.

This writer received Catholic training as a youth, but comes from a much more casual Catholic tradition where religion is not unlike dandruff —every one has a little, spends some time and money on it, but otherwise doesn't think very much about it. The depth of faith and devotion that brings barefoot pilgrims hundreds of miles on foot and drives them to their knees to ascend the steps of the church is a marvel to me not unlike the mysteries of *la Negrita's* miraculous disappearances.

The Bible tells us that faith is the substance of things hoped for and the evidence of things unseen. If that is so, there is a great deal of both substance and evidence in Cartago on August 2. As an act of faith, I'll be driving over to the basilica today to see for myself if *la Negrita* is still there. I'll have a little sip from the river, too, maybe rub some on my arthritic joints, looking for a little substance of things I hope for, a little evidence of things I can't see.

America's Global War on Sin Continues

U ncle Sam last week showed the world how he intends to protect Americans from the evils of internet wagering. Choices included regulation by the states, nationwide regulation by the feds, or prohibition. Predictably, the government is taking the path of maximum coercion and bureaucratic benefit: prohibition. Consequently, the opening gambit in the Justice Department's move against the evils of gambling looked a lot like a typically sordid day in the Drug War, or like the start of a gang war, except the other gang doesn't have guns.

American sin warriors ambushed and kidnapped the boss of a huge online sports book as he was changing planes in Dallas, Texas. In true gangland style, DOJ also grabbed a few of his relatives and business associates who made the mistake of living in the U.S.

All were charged with conspiracy and fraud for breaking an American law against taking bets over the phone. The Justice Department has also moved to extort several billion dollars in taxes it claims the company was supposed to have collected on the forbidden activity.

The busted CEO, David Carruthers, was an outspoken advocate of reasonable regulation of the gambling industry. Clearly, the DOJ also wants to confirm the wisdom of keeping your mouth shut about public policy. Carruthers admits what his company does would be a crime in the U.S.

But his company, BetonSports.com, and as many as 200 others like it, is located in Costa Rica, and therefore outside U.S. jurisdiction. If we extend the logic of Carruthers' arrest, all the thousands of employees of these companies and all of their millions of U.S. customers are criminals who should be in jail for the protection of the nation's morals.

Carruther's arrest comes just a week after the House of Representatives voted to make millions of Americans criminals. Congress passed a bill, which now awaits Senate approval, declaring internet gambling illegal. If the Senate agrees, suddenly millions of Americans who play casino games on the internet will be subject to arrest and prosecution. The bureaucratically profitable possibilities for warrantless searches, asset seizures and prison terms will jump dramatically at the stroke of a politician's pen, as will the potential for ruining innocent lives.

You would think the obvious failures of the War on Drugs, the War on Poverty and our various Wars on Penniless Peasants would warn us off a War on Gambling. That is because you do not understand the seamless bureaucratic logic of wars against sin and evil.

From the point of view of a professional sin and evil fighter, the ideal war is unwinnable. Wars that can never be won offer solid job security to the warriors and members of the support industries in the legal profession, courts, and prisons. All who fight evil prosper on ever larger budgets and wildly profitable property seizures.

The prohibition of gambling, like that of drugs, is based on the idea that some who gamble will become hopelessly addicted and ruin their lives. Therefore, everyone must take the cure. And indeed, a predictable minority of gamblers will become pathologically addicted to wagering. But that will happen whether gambling is legal or not, just as drug addiction and alcoholism occur whether drugs and alcohol are legal or not.

The image we are offered to justify another sin war is a fraud. The desperate gambler wagering the kids' lunch money on one more roll of the dice misrepresents the real profile of the casino gambler. Surveys show casino customers are better educated and better off financially than the average American. In fact, the most likely place to find the desperate welfare mom squandering the grocery money is on a state run lottery.

This is not to make light of the genuine misery caused by pathological gambling. But as with alcohol abuse, the cure is voluntary treatment, not prohibition. It's ridiculous to think compulsive gamblers won't find someplace to gamble if gambling is outlawed. Prohibition of gambling, like the prohibition of other sins, will ruin many more lives through criminal prosecution than will ever be lost to addiction.

Legally prohibiting gambling will be no more successful than other prohibitions of bad habits have been. Forbidding gambling will, however, feed parasitic enforcement organizations and ruin many more lives than it saves. Another war against sin and evil will only lead us further down the path to bureaucratic Paradise, where everything that is not prohibited is mandatory.

A Thousand Toys

Danielito, Little Danny in English, is just over three feet tall and he travels light. In this climate, you don't need much. Ten degrees north of the equator, it's never cold. Wet sometimes, but not cold. Danielito wears an orange and blue striped soccer jersey, number 14, denim shorts with pockets, dark blue low cut tennis shoes, one brown sock, one red. His hair is cut like mine, buzzed down short. You can't see scalp through his. Danny's eyes are too black to make out pupils. When he walks he pops up on his toes before each step and his arms spend a lot of time away from his body.

In his pockets and an old cookie box, he's got what he needs for the three hours he will be here. The box is yellow and bears the Spanish slogan, *Muuuuuuucha galleta*, a lot of cookie, as if it were written "a laaaaaahhhhhht of cookie."

The box contains no cookies. In it are five heavily worn, capped markers of different colors. Only four of them write, he explains. The light blue one is dried out, but he's keeping it anyway. The yellow, black, green and red still write very nicely. "Want to see?" *¿Desea ver?* His perfect Spanish accent dazzles me. I get him some paper so he can show me. Sure enough, they all work. At my request he draws a black and red cow.

Cows are a frequent topic of our conversations. I practice my Spanish on Danielito with simple sentences, uncomplicated by changing subjects. It's the *vacas*, the cows, that eat, run, dance, and sing in my Spanish chats with him. We share an appreciation for unlikely bovine activity. The only thing more comical than dancing cows is my occasional thoughtless reference to my wife as *mi esposo*, the masculine form of "my spouse."

Mismatched gender references are the height of hilarity for Latin four year olds. I keep him in stitches incorrectly guessing the unpredictable gender of such items as televisions, chairs and computers. Why or whether a table is feminine and a telephone masculine I don't know, but Danny knows and he delights in telling you.

Along with his markers, Danny also carries two plastic creatures, one a reptilian biped, green with a purple dorsal fin running to the end of a long tail. The tail curls up nicely to lend the figure a third point of support while standing. It hunches forward and holds a silver pole weapon horizontally across its body. One end of the pole sports a double bladed ax, the other a spear point. The red-eyed lizard grins, showing pointed silver teeth. His expression is unreadable, menace and goofy glee struggle to a draw on its plastic face.

The other figure is the lizard's opponent. He is clad head to toe in shiny red articulated armor and carries no weapon. His right hand forms an empty cylindrical hole where he once held something—a sword, a gun, an umbrella, flag of truce, who knows? The face is a featureless, solid slab of silver. It's a mask, Danny explains. He tells me something else about the red guy's face, but says it too fast for my skill with his language. I'm not sure if it was ruined in a fire or looks exactly like Cary Grant.

Testing the limits of my Spanish I ask how the red guy fights the lizard without weapons? Displaying great patience with the pitiful old *gringo* and making me suspect that the peaceful nature of the Costa Ricans may be genetic Danielito replies, *"No necesita armas."* He doesn't need weapons. *"Es muy fuerte."* He is very strong.

It also won't hurt the red guy that he is twice as big as the lizard, but I'm suitably impressed never the less.

Danny produces a glass marble from his pocket. Under his noisy direction, with non-stop, high-pitched commentary, including an occasional goooooooooooooaaaaaal, the two plastic figures play soccer with the marble.

"What do you call that thing," I ask, referring to the marble. *"Una bola,"* he says, astonished once again at the depth of my ignorance. I should have guessed. Rooting round in his pockets he pulls out two more glass *bolas* for my approval. I admire them lavishly.

"What else have you got," I ask. He has just one more treasure, a little plastic box with a red bottom and a scratched clear lid, the kind that snaps shut with two little beads on the side opposite the hinge. In it are a brown button and three common pins. I ask him, "What do you do with the pins?"

His reply made me think he must not be watching enough television: *"Un perno es mil juguetes."* A pin is a thousand toys.

Comida

C *omida* is the Spanish word for food. Here in Costa Rica, for hustlers and the truly destitute alike, *comida* is high on the list of magic words used to pry coins from *gringo* pockets.

The locals peg me for a *gringo* so fast you would think I was wearing a Stars and Stripes top hat. They often skip the formality of testing my Spanish and launch right into thin, broken English before I open my mouth. At street fairs the guys running the numbers games light up like kids at Christmas when they see me. Beggars find me in a crowd.

An obvious North American walking about in the capital of Costa Rica, as in other big cities, cannot give money to every beggar who asks for it. If he does he will soon be like a Pied Piper leading of a platoon of beggars. The conventional wisdom is that every *gringo* is rich as Croesus.

A heart of stone isn't the only solution, but some standards are helpful. A longtime expat offered me his advice. First, he doesn't give money to the able bodied. That he is often cursed for it, often in English, confirms what he hopes is good judgment.

He told me he also tries to support the many single-product, mobile entrepreneurs. Pens, cards, cookies, coconuts, avocados, wild flowers . . . there's a free market in street vending, fueled by pocket change, that supports a lot of hardworking people. As a free market fanatic, I love this strategy.

One of the toughest calls to make in downtown San José is to decide which children begging for food are really just hustlers. A request for "money for food" is often a request for money for DVD's and designer sunglasses. Distinguishing between the hungry and the hustler is a challenge. My expat pal suggests offering food only. If the offer is declined, how hungry could the kid be? When it's money or nothing, he recommends nothing.

I recently got to test his system in a part of town where the test was unexpected. I had just picked my sons up after school and driven across town for a piano lesson. The teacher's house is in a good neighborhood in San José, a suburb without the downtown grittiness. The American embassy is there. President Arias lives nearby.

My boys are 13 and 14 and always hungry after school. With time to kill before the lesson, we were sitting on the covered patio of a small bakery. They were tucking into apple tarts and pastry. Their less-than-buff dad was not eating, trying not to stare.

The neighborhood looked prosperous. The street was clean. The bakery faced a private pre-school, cheerfully painted in primary colors. Next door was a veterinarian's office, with a doggie salon, no less. There are no poodle groomers in real third world countries. On the corner a modern illuminated sign advertised cosmetic dentistry.

But even here, near the President's home, the array of security bars and razor wire is a reminder that neither prosperity nor honesty is universal.

The porch we sat on was three or four steps above the sidewalk. A little boy and his slightly older sister walked up in front of it. The boy's chin was at floor height. He stopped and looked up at us with bright, coal black eyes. He had a round face and dark hair buzzed down close to his head. His face and hands were dirty. His clothes, what I could see of them, were even dirtier. I noticed later he wore no shoes. The older sister stopped just out of sight past the edge of the patio. He kept looking over to her and back to us.

He mumbled something in Spanish. I looked to my younger son, Ryan, who is picking up the language a lot faster than the rest of us, for a translation. "*Comida,*" Ryan said. The magic word. Ryan said it just like the locals do, making the "d" sound something like a "th" does in English.

"He can have this, Dad," he added, offering the pastry he had half consumed. Ryan loves pastry.

That he was so quick to give up something he loves and his certainty we weren't being hustled settled the issue for me. There was no question these kids would pass the expat's test.

I went back into the bakery for sandwiches, pastries and orange juice. I offered the bag to the boy through the railing. He hesitated and looked up astonished, suspicious of the old fart—very likely a *gringo loco*. His hesitation gave way to disbelief at his good fortune. A preference for cash was never an issue. "*Gracias, señor,*" he said. He and his sister had the *comida* out of the bag before they reached the corner.

Poodle salons or not, Costa Rica still has a few miles to go to the first world.

Goliath Wins, David Deserves To

A gainst long odds, tiny Costa Rica has a team playing in the *Copa Mundial*, soccer's World Cup. Twenty-five or thirty of us had gathered at the Amistad Institute to watch the opening game. We all wore red soccer jerseys and big smiles. Excitement ran high.

Our Spanish tutor had invited us to join a group of locals and *gringo* Spanish students to watch the big game. He told us to come hungry. There would be a big *tico* breakfast. Because of the time difference between Costa Rica and the host country, Germany, the game started at ten in the morning.

The age range of the group was from less than a year to over 60, but was heavily concentrated on the sunny side of 30. We ate breakfast with gusto and spoke loud Spanglish over Latin dance music. The meal was typical Costa Rican—delicious coffee, baked plantains, and the national dish, *gallo pinto*, (literally, speckled cock, but, in fact, the timeless combo of beans and rice.) A young *tica* circulated among us painting *banderas*, little blue, white and red flags, on our cheeks.

Calling Costa Ricans crazy for soccer downplays their enthusiasm. The national soccer team, nicknamed *Los Ticos*, was in the *Copa Mundial* for only the third time in history. It's a HUGE national event. There is no American sports equivalent. The Super Bowl might come close, but even that is a national, not a global, event. And it happens every year. The World Cup, like the Olympics, only comes around every four years.

For a small country of rabid soccer fans, the national team playing in the World Cup is at least as important as an election. Winning it would be the competitive equivalent of the Second Coming.

The morning of the game would have been the perfect time for a bank heist in San José. The country was shut down. Schools were out. Offices were closed. And for good reason—*los Ticos* had the honor of playing the opening game of the *Mundial* against soccer powerhouse and tournament host Germany.

The two countries could hardly be more different. David was more evenly matched with Goliath. There are twenty times as many Germans as Costa Ricans. The Germans have played in every World Cup since 1954. They are three time champions. Costa Rica's only other appearances at the tourney were in 1990 and 2002. In their best finish they made it to the second round.

And perhaps, in even more telling contrast, while much of the world remains wary of warlike, industrial Germany, it can only marvel at unarmed, unassuming Costa Rica—peacefully honoring its national motto, *Pura Vida*, pure life, even in the midst of murderous local wars.

The small chance of a Costa Rican championship did nothing to dampen local team spirit. Our little group sang the Costa Rican national anthem with verve and volume, adding a verse beyond the pitifully short rendition at the tournament. They started cheering when the players were introduced and continued throughout the game, pausing only briefly after each German goal.

Soccer chants were nearly continuous after the kick-off. "*TICOS, oooohaaaaayooooohaaaaaa-yooooohaaaaaay!*" rang through the neighborhood. There were half a dozen others I could only get half the words for. They shouted urgent instructions in staccato Spanish to our players, who mostly ignored the advice. They bitterly protested penalties against *los Ticos* and received those against the Germans with the satisfaction of the righteous.

Less than a minute into the game a German player got off a shot like a cannonball from 50 yards out. It missed by a hair over the top bar catching the outside of the net. At first it looked like a devastating, impossibly long range goal, impossibly early in the game. The prospect of a humiliating defeat passed over the room in silence, like the shadow of a hawk over a robin's nest. We bounced back quickly, however, when we realized there was no goal. Chanting and cheering resumed at full volume.

Los Ticos were hard pressed from the start. Heroic saves held the Germans to one goal in the first 30 minutes. The *Tico's* star striker tied it up when he scored on the only shot the team would make in the first half. I thought the roof would come off the building. The dancing and chanting continued through half time.

The German team was faster and more precise. They had the ball most of the time. The Costa Ricans defended like tigers in the second half and scored a second goal on a lucky break away. The final score was 4 to 2. Goliath was too much for David, but David was no pushover. The defeat didn't dampen the spirits of our little group. *Los Ticos* had played nobly. They'd done their country proud.

And the Costa Rican fans, with warmth, good humor and *pura vida* spirit, had once again shown their *gringo* guests what their country shows the world all the time.

If you can't always win, you can deserve to win.

Preventive Medicine

Shortly after I turned 50, I had a medical checkup in Key West. I remember only one specific piece of information the doctor gave me during that exam. He said, "There is no reason anyone should ever die of colon cancer." An annual preventive colonoscopy would detect most potentially dangerous tumors before they became serious. The doctor planned to have an endoscopic exam himself every year.

His remark impressed me because genetically I'm in a group whose members too often draw the short straw for cancer. My father's uncle died of colon cancer at age 43. Two more of my grandmother's siblings also died of cancer in their fifties. My sister, at 41, is an eight year cancer survivor, and happily, enjoying a remission. My father developed lung cancer at 56, my age now. He survived 13 more years on one lung, stubbornness, and an ironic sense of humor.

The chances of my having a winning ticket in the cancer lottery should have put me on the colonoscopy bandwagon long ago. But it didn't. Apart from the obvious reasons to put it off, there is another. Whether it's also a genetic flaw I do not know, but I'm an insufferable tightwad. When I discovered the procedure in Key West cost something north of $5,000 I kept finding excuses to wait.

Five thousand bucks! The insurance policy I was paying $8,000 a year for wouldn't cover any part of it—unless I already had cancer. The company promised up to a million dollars for treatment, but not a cent for prevention. Go figure.

In the five years since my 50 year exam I've saved $25,000 and avoided seeing my GI tract on TV, but at the risk of wishing I'd spent the money.

Now I'm living in Costa Rica. Medical care here is first class. Private and public systems run side by side. A private doctor's visit cost me $40. I waited less than a week for it. That doctor, not surprisingly, recommended an annual preventive colonoscopy.

I scheduled one. I called for an appointment around noon on a Thursday. I was stunned when the doctor asked me if I had eaten breakfast that morning. If I hadn't, he was going to do the exam the next day. When I reported my *huevos* and *tortillas* he scheduled me for the following Monday. He told me how to get ready.

"How much will it cost?" I asked. "110,000 *colones*," he said, about $220.

It would take about an hour from arrival to departure. I would have to buy my own laxative. Another $10 down the tubes, so to speak. This brings me to another advantage of having a colonoscopy in a second language. If your Spanish is bad enough, as mine surely is, embarrassment vanishes in the fog of linguistic confusion. Asking a pretty woman for a few doses of a laxative powerful enough to purge a water buffalo caused me not the slightest unease. I was too busy trying to understand her answer.

The procedure took place in the doctor's office on the 7th floor of a modern clinic. I was 10 minutes late. We began immediately. The small consulting room was clean and new, lined with modern electronic gear and staffed by two typically friendly and perfectly lovely Costa Rican nurses. They spoke enough English to get me checked in with a minimum of embarrassment and confusion. When my Spanish collapsed, the doctor spoke fluent English. Even at less than a 20th of the cost of the same procedure in Key West, I didn't notice any scrimping or cut corners.

They knocked me out without any fuss. I awoke less than an hour later with some cramps and no memory of the procedure. My wife was thrilled she got to watch the whole thing.

The after-effects were limited to a few spectacular farts. In 15 minutes I was on my way home with a dozen hi-res color photos taken inside my never-before-seen, looks-as-good-as-new large intestine.

So why do you pay 10 to 20 times more for the same hour's work in the U.S.? I can think of a few reasons.

Separate public and private health care systems in CR means very few third party payers and even fewer costly regulations in the private system.

Without insurance, private patients do not suddenly become rich as Croesus when their bill reaches the magic "deductible" number. Demand is limited by common sense rather than the limits of gold plated insurance policies. Preventive medicine is cost effective. People spending their own money are always more careful with it. It helps keep prices reasonable.

And then there's the legal system. Contingency lawsuits are unknown here. You can't just sue a doctor and expect a settlement because it's cheaper to pay than fight. Sue and lose and you pay for everything. In the States we have a lawyer for every 275 people. If we just include working adults, there are only about 100 to support each attorney. By comparison, tort lawyers are thin on the ground here. The money Costa Ricans save on law suits alone buys a lot of medical care.

It's no wonder *ticos* live so long. They can afford to.

Filling the Gap

*"Politics is the gentle art of getting votes from the
poor and campaign funds from the rich by
promising to protect each from the other."*
— Oscar Ameringer

"Gap Grows Between Rich, Poor" hollered the headline in the *Tico Times*. It could have said "Costa Rican Income Doubles" if the editors had chosen to see the glass half full. Despite the headline, the report contained a lot of good news.

Costa Rica is richer than it was in 1988. Other things being equal, prosperity is good. Poverty is bad. Once you get used to them, clean water, electricity, and refrigeration are not luxuries.

The *Tico Times* led with the bad news, however. The poorest fifth of the population was not any better off than it was 15 years ago. That is bad news indeed, for everyone but politicians. It's the kind of bad news that manures the rolling fields of envy and resentment where socialists harvest their votes. Over 50 years of socialism in this country and the poor are still dirt poor. The government must need more money.

Not surprisingly, Costa Rica's socialist president quickly suggested just that. If he could just mow down the tallest plants in that field he could end poverty and corruption and fill the pot holes. But everybody here knows, after tossing a few clippings down to the have-nots, the mowers themselves consume most of the harvest.

Socialism has a powerful philosophical appeal and an attractive, if larcenous, logic. It also features delicious irony. Despite wide agreement that theft is immoral, electing a thief who promises to split his loot with those who elect him delivers both the voters and the thief to unassailable moral high ground.

The idea of soaking the rich to help the poor supports political bureaucracies all over the globe. Democracy is held in such reverence that the morality of three lions and a zebra voting on what's for dinner is never questioned. Garden-variety socialists believe that taking wealth from those who produce it and giving it to those who vote for it makes the world a better place.

And if brilliant, incorruptible angels administered socialist governments, the world would surely improve. Unfortunately, governments are run by politicians and their camp followers—people lacking any credible claim to superior intelligence, competence, or character.

This group is the political class. It neither sows nor reaps. It lives on wealth taxed away from the productive economy. Few members have the remotest idea of how wealth is produced, but all know where their bread is buttered.

Success in the private sector depends on hard work, innovation, productivity, and, ultimately, giving good value to customers.

Success in the political economy depends on lording it over as many people as possible, sucking up to the powerful, and transferring loot from foes to friends. The widespread faith that players in the political economy can or even want to improve the world is one of life's great mysteries.

The political class thrives in the fertile valley between the rich and the poor. The wider the gap the greater is the opportunity to leap to the controls of the rumbling bulldozer of social democracy. That is why the political class, despite loudly deploring the growing gulf between haves and have-nots, can only widen it.

To understand how this is so we must understand how people get rich. Keynesian hoo-haw about the "paradox of thrift" aside, you can't spend yourself rich. Borrowing money to buy stuff you don't need may provide years of riotous fun, but it's like burning the furniture to heat your living room. Eventually you'll be sitting on the floor, shivering in the dark.

To become richer, people and nations must produce more than they consume. They must then wisely invest the difference to increase productivity. Investments in tools, machinery or research produce more wealth.

A man with a shovel moves more dirt than a guy digging with his bare hands. A man with a backhoe moves more still, but before they can reap the benefits of power digging, they must save enough of what they earned with their bare hands to buy the shovel or the backhoe. The added productivity, and their greater prosperity, is the return on the savings invested in the tools.

Socialist governments take money from productive members of society but they do not invest it. They consume it or give it to others who consume it. At the same time, by inflating the currency, they quietly confiscate society's savings. The confiscation hurts the poorest the most. It prevents them from accumulating capital. It steals their past labor, and thus steals their future productivity. It keeps them from ever saving enough to buy tools, whether the tool is a shovel or a college degree.

Countries like Costa Rica routinely devalue their currency by 10% to 20% a year. If you are making $500 a month, which would be a big raise for the poorest families here, anything you save will be confiscated through inflation. You will never accumulate the capital necessary to escape your poverty. The government that claims to work for your benefit conspires to keep you poor and dependent, by stealing your savings with inflation.

At the same time, the wealth siphoned off the productive economy will never be invested in the factories or machinery that could provide a poor person with a better, more productive job. That wealth will be squandered in "administrative costs" or used to buy votes.

Governments can increase the prosperity of their people. They can do it by providing a stable, honest currency, by protecting the rights of every citizen, and by keeping down the number of freeloaders on the gravy train.

Everything else government does just adds to the load the productive economy must bear and keeps the poorest very poor indeed. The gap between rich and poor will never be closed by filling it with politicians and paper pushers.

Education or Indoctrination

"There are two distinct classes of men . . . those who pay taxes and those who receive and live upon taxes." — Thomas Paine

L iving in a shamelessly socialist country I am occasionally surprised by the candor of members of the local tax consuming class even if they do fall far short of the truth of Thomas Paine's remark above. Paine's insight tends to erode willing participation by the mules pulling the gravy train. Nevertheless, Costa Rican bureaucrats often let slip truths that would be hooted down if made by a U.S. counterpart.

Today, the online English newspaper, *A.M. Costa Rica*, ran an article about the *Systema de Tecnología de Información para el Control Aduaneroa* (say that three times fast), the new import tax system. TICA for short. The acronym is also the local slang for a Costa Rican woman. Cute, eh?

The new system is a high tech effort to collect more taxes. There is great economic incentive to avoid Costa Rican import duties because they are consistently high, as much as 100% on many items. The techno system is the latest escalation in the battle between smuggler and tax collector.

Much of the article reads like a press release from the Customs Bureau. It described a new Techno Bus now wandering the country to train customs agents in the latest tax collection techniques. What struck this reader, however, was the revelation that the bus is not *only* for training customs agents.

"The bus also will be used to indoctrinate school children in the need to pay taxes. This is one of the big projects that the *Ministerio de Hacienda* plans for the next administration, to create a spirit of cooperation among young people so they will willingly pay taxes."

The customs department is an agency of *Hacienda*. It seems the department is moving briskly into the new millennium with high tech tracking gear that will assure that nothing enters the country unmonitored or untaxed.

In other words, the government wants to train the sheep to step up proudly for shearing. The idea doesn't bother anyone. That's the kind of candor you will never hear from agents of stealth socialism in the States. The IRS, for instance, will never tell us that one of their big plans this year will be to brainwash our children into becoming obedient taxpayers. We will never hear that a program like DARE is an official effort to weaken family loyalty and create a generation of snitches in the hopeless but irresistibly lucrative drug war. At least we can admire the honesty of true socialists.

The Costa Ricans are a naturally peaceful people. I've occasionally noticed an almost crippling politeness. *Ticos* often making promises they know they will not keep to avoid hurting your feelings. They take childhood indoctrination for granted. They don't seem to mind. It doesn't bother them that no item arriving in the country will escape a crushing import duty. Perhaps it's because they have been so thoroughly indoctrinated themselves. Perhaps it is because they know that many items will arrive untaxed through informal channels.

Like the Costa Rican customs office, government institutions everywhere have an educational agenda. They are neither interested in nor systemically capable of teaching independent thinking. Here, at least, the socialist institutions are honest about their goals. Indoctrination, not education is the object. A country of obedient taxpayers is greatly to be preferred over a country of independent individualists.

My native country, on the on the other hand, has slipped into an unnamed, stealth socialism that is at odds with our traditions and what we believe to be our national character. Powerful tax consuming groups like teachers and other public employee unions have reaped huge benefits from a coercive system. What we've gotten in return is a poorly educated but thoroughly indoctrinated herd of taxpaying sheep.

Public education is the chief vehicle of indoctrination. Like all government undertakings, it is coercive from top to bottom. The law forces students to go to school. The law forces taxpayers to pay for it. Teachers and administrators are all paid with these taxes. Government employees decide every detail of the curriculum.

Children are institutionalized in public schools as early as age four. They spend more time in school than most convicted violent felons spend in prison. Many, and particularly boys, receive powerful psychoactive drugs to control their behavior. All begin each day by taking a government approved loyalty oath.

Such an environment will not produce adults with a healthy mistrust of official power. A curriculum produced and presented by government employees will never wander far from the smooth, straight path of naive trust and solemn reverence for authority. It will never wander far from indoctrination.

When students fail on test after test the call goes out for more money to better teach the basics. When will we recognize it as simply a call for more money? Greater government involvement in education will only intensify ignorance and strengthen trust in official authority. Programs like No Child Left Behind are quickly morphing into No Child Left Unpsychoanalyzed, No Child

Left Undrugged, and ultimately No Child Left to Think for Himself.

If we are going to train ourselves to be obedient taxpayers, the least we can do is be honest about it. Government bureaucrats can only indoctrinate, not educate.

Promoting Mass Murder

"The strongest reason for the people to retain the right to keep and bear arms is, as a last resort, to protect themselves against tyranny in government."
— *Thomas Jefferson*

Costa Rica has no military. Private firearms are registered and strictly controlled, although not difficult to get. Oscar Arias, Nobel Peace Prize winner and president elect of Costa Rica, giving little credit to the civic character of his countrymen, thinks this is why Costa Rica is such a peaceful country.

Mr. Arias recently attended a UN confab dedicated to making sure only government employees have guns. He has declared himself in favor of the UN's efforts toward civilian disarmament. Mr. Arias is rich, famous, and popular, and I'm sure he's well-intentioned, but he's wrong about guns.

He won the Nobel Prize in 1987 for his efforts in brokering a peace deal between the Sandinistas and the U.S. supported "Contras" in Nicaragua. After he won the prize everyone but the prize committee ignored the plan. The war didn't end until 1992.

It's hard to believe Mr. Arias is so naive that he thinks armed civilians were the cause of Central American wars. He and everyone familiar with the brutal civil wars fought in El Salvador, Nicaragua and Guatemala during the '70s and '80s knows the worst atrocities, murders, and massacres were carried out by armed government agents against unarmed civilians. The U.S. government supported and supplied the murderous governments in every case. Government soldiers and agents murdered thousands of innocent civilians, many more than armed criminals ever will or could.

The UN, the same outfit that is now so keen to make sure civilians don't have guns, confirmed that fact in its 1993 "Truth Commission Report." The report said that over 96% of "human rights violations" (UN-speak for rapes and murders) were committed by military or quasi-military death squads against unarmed civilians.

Naturally, the UN report has been criticized as a highly political document. It surely is. But even if the report is as political as Kofi Annan's rolodex, there were still a lot of innocent, unarmed people killed by government agents in Central America.

In El Salvador alone over 75,000 mostly un-armed people were killed mostly by government employees between 1980 and 1992. By 20th century massacre standards, that's not a big number, but it devastated tiny El Salvador. If a similar percentage of the U.S. population had perished, the death toll would have been 4.2 million.

With shameless and generally unreported help from the USA, the governments of Nicaragua and Guatemala also murdered tens of thousand of their unarmed citizens during these same years. Millions more have died in this century at the hands of armed governments who have first disarmed their citizens. Judging by the UN's own report, promoting civilian disarmament amounts to promoting mass murder.

The UN frames the issue in terms of public safety, but public safety arguments ignore the greater danger. While there is no question that some weapons left over from the wars in Central America are now used in crimes, the fact remains that all the crimes committed by all the criminals in history haven't claimed a tiny fraction of the number lives lost to criminal governments.

If Pancho and Juan start shooting up the town or even if they set up a roadblock and shake down tourists, they will never be as dangerous as a battalion of trained goons intent on wiping out whole families, villages, or political groups. If everyone in town has a gun, Pancho, Juan, and the goons will have a lot harder time hurting anyone.

Every one of the many genocides, massacres, and ethnic cleansings conducted in the last century has been conducted against a populace that was forbidden ownership of firearms. If Mr. Arias were really concerned about the welfare and prosperity of his people he wouldn't be calling for their disarmament. He would instead insist on providing every able bodied citizen a rifle, ammunition and training in their use.

The Swiss government does exactly that. Switzerland is a wonderfully peaceful and pleasant place to live. There is not much crime. There's never been a genocide. The Swiss have enjoyed peace for over 150 years even as neighboring governments have slaughtered millions. Crime will remain low and mass murder will remain impossible as long as Swiss citizens remain armed. Mr. Arias should take note and stop promoting mass murder.

A Modest Proposal for New Tax Laws

As a newcomer I'm having some trouble distinguishing between the political parties here in Costa Rica. Although there are many more of them here than there are in the States, there are just two that matter. Just like in the States, the difference between the two is obvious only to party members. To an outsider, like this writer, there is practically no difference. The primary mission of both parties is to take wealth from the productive economy and use the money to buy political support.

The Costa Rican government runs like most modern democracies: it spends more money than it takes in. It borrows the difference. It then swindles lenders and locals alike by printing truckloads of the local monetary tokens, called *colones* (rhymes with baloneys when spoken by *gringos*). The government then repays lenders and buys votes with the rapidly depreciating paper tokens.

After years of spending more than they take in, printing more money won't keep up. Both leading political parties agree it's time for a massive tax increase. The 57 member legislature is squabbling over the final details of a law that they gleefully project will net the political class an extra $500 million a year, about 12% of annual spending. Supporting politicians speak of the urgent need for the $500 mill as though each supporting voter will receive the full amount in cash the moment the law passes.

That figure is small potatoes by the standards of the Empire of IOU's, but this is a small country. The population is roughly that of South Carolina. They live in an area about the size of Vermont. Total annual spending by the Costa Rican central government would fund the U.S. Defense Department for less than three days. Luckily for the Costa Ricans, their government doesn't spend anything on defense. They have no military.

That is not to say the Costa Rican government doesn't squander tax money, however. They simply don't squander it on bombs and bullets. The Costa Ricans have a peaceful army of paper pushers. From what I can see that army's main job is to keep people waiting in long lines to pay small sums and have pieces of paper officially stamped.

The new tax law promises to increase the size of that army substantially. To the political organizations involved, of course, this is a good thing. It will mean more supporters beholden to the party for their jobs, even as it drains the life out of the economy. The new law will change the current 13% sales tax on retail sales to a smaller, less visible Value Added Tax that will be levied at every level of the economy.

That scheme dragoons every business in the country into the tax collection game instead of just retailers. It also creates more complex bookkeeping requirements. Tax will be due only on the value added above the costs of production. The producer will then simply include the new tax in his final selling price.

Because price increases that don't yield more profit make products less competitive, there will be a powerful incentive to under report added value. A value added tax scheme will provide a rich fertilizer to broad fields of creative accounting while requiring a much larger enforcement effort.

The Costa Ricans have also consulted American's favorite bureaucracy, the IRS, for advice on taxing citizens and resident foreigners who earn money outside Costa Rica. (They already tax money earned inside the country.) Without ever considering why Americans might find Costa Rica attractive, the legislature thinks taxing worldwide income is a swell idea. Like lawmakers everywhere they predict their take based on what is called "static analysis." Static analysis assumes that no one will change the way they do business because of the new tax.

The failed U.S. tax on luxury items like yachts and expensive cars in the '90s is a good example. Congress slapped a 10% excise on luxury goods. Congress expected to collect many millions in new revenue from rich guys buying yachts and Porches. Instead many fewer luxury cars and yachts were sold. Several U.S. yacht makers went out of business throwing taxpaying, middle-class wage earners out of work. When you figure in the lost payroll taxes, the new tax was a dead loss.

Costa Rican legislators are probably no more venal and corrupt than legislators elsewhere. Costa Rican bureaucrats are probably no more incompetent than other bureaucrats. But in a country where maintenance consists of replacing bridges years after they collapse into the river, a complex new scheme for collecting taxes is not likely to extract any greater wealth from the economy than the current leaky system does.

I have a suggestion that I believe may keep Costa Rica and other democracies from plunging into a morass of new tax rules for no good reason. It was inspired by a photo of a single copy of the law that appeared in the San José daily, *La Nacion*. The photo showed the new bill sitting on the floor next to a wall. Side by side stacks of paper about two feet high, bound roughly in clumps of 500 pages, stretched off along the wall out of sight. Twelve two-foot high stacks were visible, but there was clearly more paper in the distance.

My suggestion is this, before passing a law, simply require the legislators, working in shifts if necessary, to read the new tax law aloud into the record during regular legislative sessions. In many cases that would take several years. Our leaders would probably give up or have to seek re-election before any real damage is done.

Spanish Lesson

With an hour to kill, I slid my ample *gringo* butt onto the low stone wall. The stone was polished smooth by thousands of butts before mine. There were benches, too. People sat on them alone or in pairs, and on the walls. Massive trees cast a thick shade.

I was at the southwest corner of *Parque Central*, in San José, Costa Rica. The square features a massive band stand in the center, covered by a vaulting wedding cake gazebo in cranberry red and pigeon dung white. There's a life-sized bronze statue of a guy sweeping up a pile of bronze litter. The real litter receives less diligent attention. A broad cathedral spans the whole block on the east side of the plaza. Midday sunlight exploded off its flat white facade lighting the shade of my corner without heating it.

The ground rose from my wall toward the church. The rise began with three broad steps a few feet in front of me. At the top of those steps a man was preaching in a loud, strong baritone.

He was short and dark, almost swarthy, with a square jaw and white, straight teeth. He dressed plainly in clean, colorless clothes. His no-nonsense work shoes were shined. From under a thatch of glossy dark hair his black eyes scanned the crowd for lost souls. He proclaimed the glory of *Jesús Cristo* in a strong baritone.

He held a small black Bible in his left hand. A battered blue metal toolbox was on the ground at his feet. As he spoke, he paced a few steps away from it and back, chopping the air with his right arm as he spoke. His voice carried clearly over the noise of the traffic. To my untrained ear he spoke wonderful Spanish.

The Spanish language is still largely incomprehensible to me, though I strive daily to learn it. Here I had stumbled on a chance for a live Spanish lesson. Right away I could pick out a few words. He spoke as I so often ask locals to speak to me—slowly and distinctly, as if to an imbecile.

The preacher spoke Spanish the way I do in my dreams—like Antonio Banderas coaxing a dark eyed beauty out of her lacy shift, or Richardo Montalban admiring "reech Corrreenthian leyther" in his native language.

His r's rolled deliciously, not with the exaggerated flutter of the soccer announcers, but with the warm roundness of good red wine in a big glass. He pronounced d's with that smooth, mysterious not-quite-a-lisp that makes words sound like the speaker is smiling.

As the sound of his voice washed over me, the preacher's words carried me along despite my incomprehension. He was riveting. He spoke with passion and power. He was smooth and articulate. He switched seamlessly from the Bible to his own words. The people sitting scattered around him rarely looked at him, as though pretending not to listen. But they were sitting there for the same reason I was, to hear the preacher.

He spoke with a hypnotic rhythm, repeating simple verbs and nouns. I began to pick out phrases as they came around again and again like the refrain in a hymn. I understood just enough to recognize the timeless themes. *Amor* . . . Love. *Muerte* . . . Death. *Vida* . . . Life. *Pecado* . . . Sin. The multisyllabic Spanish softened and romanticized the hard Anglo-Saxon—sins became wonderfully trivial *pecados*. Amen to that, *amigos*. You can count on the romance of a romance language.

The preacher kept talking and pacing, away from his toolbox and back. The box looked like its two parallel handles could open left and right to expose tiers of trays. The blue paint was chipped and scratched. The centers of the handles were worn to bare metal. They shone dull silver in the shade.

I wondered what tools a preacher would lug around with him. I had visions of blessed lures, custom painted for trolling in this lake of unsaved souls, special spoons and plugs handed down from Christ's first dozen fishers. Mystical tackle passed from them to the Roman soldiers who a thousand years ago slowly turned Latin into Spanish. Spiritual tools handed finally to this preacher who now cast sparkling Latinate words into the sea of sinners in San José, trolling for souls.

His words spread out in a sacred chum slick behind the fishing boat of salvation. I imagined a golden stringer in the bottom of the box ready to bind saved souls together until it was time to take them home.

I decided to go before he opened the box. A little salvation is good for everyone, but I'm not ready to be pulled from the school of sinners just yet. His Spanish alone had drawn me up behind the boat. I feared the Holy Gaff.

Our eyes met as I left, *"Se llama Jesús Cristo,"* he said, loud and strong. He had come to his refrain with perfect timing. "His name is Jesus Christ." I wandered off mumbling to myself, trying to sound like him, carefully repeating Spanish words of hope and redemption.

School Days

At ages 13 and 14 our boys attended their first day of school today. It wasn't their first day of reading and math, but it was their first day of school as most of us think of school. Rows of desks. A teacher at the chalkboard. Rooms full of fellow prisoners longing for the sound of a bell.

Until our arrival in Costa Rica, except for a brief quarter in Key West's Home School High School, our boys have been schooled by me, their old man, in our home. My goals in educating them have generally been humble. I hoped to avoid having them drugged into a stupor and to equip them with the tools to get along in life as something other than gardeners for Chinese industrialists.

After a month of unrelenting togetherness during the move, and with the increasingly pressing need for their parents to earn some kind of living, something had to give. Fortunately, our choices for educating the boys here in Costa Rica are numerous and appealing.

The boys now attend the European School on a beautiful campus in the suburbs above San José. The school is owned and run by a woman dedicated to the humanities. She reminds me of the fictional Jean Brody. She is a French polyglot, dedicated, opinionated, educated, charming, certain of the righteousness of her mission. Math and science are not her priorities. Our boys will have to drop back a year or two in math to catch up in Greek mythology and Latin. It's a trade off I can live with.

What finally clinched the deal was that lunch was included in the tuition. We could break even with what we save on peanut butter and orange juice alone.

Most students at the European School are Costa Rican. Even though most of the students are native speakers of Spanish the entire high school curriculum is in English. All students must demonstrate fluency in both Spanish and English to graduate.

There are so many children in Costa Rica that the public schools have to teach them in shifts. The San José phone book contains hundreds of listings for private schools of all kinds. The *Ticos* have a respect for education that borders on reverence.

It is a respect that we were hard pressed to find in the states. There, we had to choose between the chaos and absurdly low standards of the public schools or the emphasis on safety that ignored curriculum at the private schools. Of course, we want our boys to feel good about themselves. But there is nothing like genuine accomplishment to boost self esteem.

The decline of education in America is reversing the global pattern of colonial times. In those days British aristocrats and American engineers spread across the world and made half hearted efforts to raise the heathens out of their ignorance. We didn't expect much of them, they being little brown people for the most part and not suited to much beyond hole digging and hedge trimming.

But the ignorant little brown people weren't paying much attention to what we thought. They studied hard while we relaxed. They are now doing calculus in their heads. They don't know any better. We now import them to do the intellectual heavy lifting as America rushes to become a third world country.

Need unscientific evidence?

Take a look the names in the faculty directory of any University Engineering Department. Names like Chen, Wang, and Suryanarayana appear in numbers all out of proportion with their appearance in a phone book.

They belong to Asian immigrants who were educated in India, China, and Japan. It's as though we Americans are deliberately dumbing ourselves down, and doing it on money we borrow from

Asians. As Asians get smarter we are preparing our children for careers as their houseboys and nannies.

Need more evidence? Even our college grads are largely as dumb as stumps. The National Assessment of Adult Literacy, which came out at the end of 2005 had this to say:

"Only 41 percent of graduate students tested in 2003 could be classified as 'proficient' in prose—reading and understanding information in short texts—down 10 percentage points since 1992. Of college graduates, only 31 percent were classified as proficient, compared with 40 percent in 1992."

They aren't talking about third graders. These are sheep-skin bearing adults. And they're not talking about plowing through Kierkegaard and Kant. The short texts were more along the lines of the "Adventures of Dick and Jane."

Yeah, maybe the research includes some of the underachievers who were passed along without regard to their work, but we are all supposed to be able to read before we leave elementary school.

Costa Rican 5th graders can read English as well as an American college grad.

The authors of the study were puzzled to explain the decline in American reading skills. But, ever willing to suggest the unpopular, I'll explain it. American reading skills are declining because American schools are run by underachieving feminist social engineers who are infinitely more interested in maintaining order than in imparting a liberal education. Reading has declined because American children are no longer taught how to read systematically with phonetics. This is in no small part because the illiterate are more compliant. Anyone can teach a child to read phonically in a few months. Wasting 10, 12, or 16 years in a series of institutions requires the skill of a true educational expert.

I hope the European School will allow me to skip coaching my boys on the finer points of using shovels and mops. There may be other opportunities as well for illiterate Americans to serve their Asian employers: house cleaning, doing laundry, and cab driving come to mind. I hope schooling outside the U.S. will allow my sons to remain unfamiliar with them all.

Volcanic Bubbles

Against all advice we arrived at night. We'd been driving for two hours in the dark through something like Jurassic Park. An impenetrable wall of vegetation lined both sides of the narrow, winding road. Lame T-Rex jokes were hilarious. Every fallen log looked like a big lizard.

At irregular intervals the pavement ended without warning and the road became a rutted gravel track. After a while, the track changed just as suddenly back to profoundly potholed pavement. It was as if the Pavement Fairy had flown over and dropped loads of precious black-top at random intervals along the way.

The road was more or less two cars wide except at all the bridges. The bridges were slightly more than one car wide. For the last half hour our aging RAV 4 crawled along in either first or second gear over a dirt road that in the U.S. would have ended at a pile of rusting refrigerators. Here it ended at a luxury resort built at the base of the very active

Arenal Volcano, in the Central Highlands of Costa Rica.

Having arrived in the dark we missed the scenery on the way in. Everyone in the car was so intent on not leaving the road or having something from beside the road eat us alive that it was as though we had come in through a leafy tunnel.

When the sun rose the next morning, it was behind a stunning pile of ashes that towered thousands of feet above the hotel. Looking up open-mouthed at the top, I had conflicting urges to run away as fast as I could and to climb to the top of it immediately.

We had managed to arrive on one of the few days when clouds and smoke didn't obscure the top of the volcano. The smoking cone stunned us into silence. It was hard to take your eyes off it. There were no TV's in the rooms. Chairs faced the windows that faced the smoldering mountain.

On a hike to a nearby waterfall we heard our first tremendous roar. We thought we were hearing jets. The sound was like a squadron of F-15's blowing by on full afterburner. But Costa Rica doesn't have an air force and the airport is 100 miles away. It's the noise the mountain makes.

At night, glowing cinders the size of Hummers cascade down from the top of the cone. They come apart as they roll down breaking into a burning, smoking, glowing cascade of lava, ashes and fire. The lava spreads like glowing sweet sauce on an ice cream sundae. Walt Disney himself couldn't have pulled the permits to build this thing.

Arenal has been active since 1968. As volcanoes go, it's not particularly dangerous. The BATF has killed more people than Arenal has. Drunk drivers are statistically way more dangerous. Never the less, there's something about close proximity to potential natural catastrophe that sharpens the senses. And, like life in the path of monster hurricanes in South Florida, there seems to be something about it that makes the land particularly desirable.

The volcano sits at one end of a huge lake. We drove some 20 miles down the north shore of that lake the next day. The roads are so bad it took over an hour to cover the distance. I expected sleepy villages, dusty farms and tiny fruterias, but what we found was a development frenzy in full cry. The volcano was the only patch of ground in the area not sporting a FOR SALE sign.

Why didn't we think of this for Iraq? We don't need tanks and planes. For the money we're spending we could have just bought the place. In the first town we came to you could speak English in any store or restaurant. Menus were in English. Prices were in dollars and about as many of them as you would expect in Florida. Every local had a friend with some land for sale.

Elsewhere I've been so far in Costa Rica there is evidence of a migrating U.S. real estate bubble, but here on the shore of Lake Arenal, the evidence is overwhelming. The similarities between this and South Florida in 2004 are striking. Prices have increased over 40% a year for the last two years. People with perfectly good jobs are quitting them to sell real estate. Buyers, almost entirely American, are in a frenzy to buy something, often anything, often sight unseen because prices will only be higher next year. And even with recent price jumps, land is cheap by American standards, and gorgeous by any standard.

Will it end any time soon? I surely don't know. The participants, like participants in all bubbles don't think it ever will. There is little borrowed money involved. Or at least the money isn't borrowed locally. Financing here is expensive when it can be had at all.

There is no evidence of speculation by those who can't afford to speculate. The gardeners, waiters and house keepers are not buying spec houses yet.

But even with the differences, I had an uncomfortable feeling that I had been someplace like this before. We headed back the next day to the suburbs of San José, eager to put a little distance between us and looming cataclysm, volcanic and otherwise. I had a powerful urge to get back to where I have trouble reading the signs and communication is an elaborate game of charades.

Geezer Power

Socialism comes in two barely distinguishable flavors here in Costa Rica, much as it does in the United States. Two socialist candidates for president are battling it out in the closest race in the country's history. One is a youngish 51 and the overwhelming favorite in the only big city in the country. The other is a 65-year-old Nobel Laureate who had to win a case in the country's constitutional court to be able to run again for president. There is a constitutional prohibition against a president serving more than one term. He was president of Cost Rica more than 15 years ago. His strength is in the countryside where he dominates in landslide proportions.

Both candidates have promised to raise taxes and end corruption. The first promise is a lock. In its attempt to allow everyone to live at everyone else's expense this government, like socialist governments everywhere, runs a chronic deficit. The local currency depreciates against the less rapidly depreciating dollar at over 10% a year. The last three zeros on the local currency are already pointless. Higher taxes or more inflation are the only choices for Costa Rican politicians locked into a spending spiral.

The second promise is a classic that only the brain dead could believe. Oscar Arias, the Nobelista and current leader, is a successful business-man who has mumbled a few words about reforming the many government monopolies that keep citizens standing in long lines throughout the country. Arias' suggestion that there might be too much paper being pushed earned him the undying enmity of the army of paper pushers employed by those monopolies.

The candle of innovation is well hidden under the basket of hundreds of government monopolies. One in seven Costa Ricans works for the government. They are, by and large, among the most prosperous citizens in the country. They are bellied up to a public trough brimming with benefits the private sector can only dream of.

At this writing, two days after the election and with about 90% of over a million votes counted, fewer than 3,500 votes separate the two front runners. That's less then two tenths of a percent of the total vote cast—less than one vote at each of the over 5,000 polling places. That's a razor thin margin in this country of 4 million souls who live in a breathtakingly beautiful, volcano-studded land about the size of West Virginia.

The Costa Rican constitution requires that the winner have at least 40% of the vote to avoid a run-off. The two leaders hover around 40.5% each right now. What is most interesting to this visiting *gringo*, who admits a thorough ignorance of local politics, is the third runner-up. The *Movimiento Libertario*, the honest-to-God, right wing wacko, Libertarian Party has most of the vote that didn't go to the two front runners.

The Libertarian party candidate, Otto Guevara, picked up over 120,000 votes out of some 1.3 million cast. If the Libertarian Party in the U.S. gleaned that much of the vote the talking heads would be choking on their lattés.

It's hard to explain. But that won't stop me from trying. Numerically I'm thinking 40% of the electorate is riding the gravy train benefiting from the government or government run monopolies, 40% get free medical care and education so they think they are winning when they are really pulling the train for the first group. The 10% that votes Libertarian are those who can't get licenses to drive cabs or open fruit stands.

The election itself is a gigantic party. They even call it the voting fiesta. Trucks stuffed with drum beating, flag waving party supporters cruise the streets honking horns, chanting and hollering for their guys. And they do it more or less sober.

To mitigate the area's historic tendencies toward *coup d'etat*, the sale of liquor is forbidden in the days immediately preceding and following

Election Day. Though such a decision might actually precipitate a coup in the U.S., it seems to work here. Even with the election as close as it is there is little indication that anyone thinks it involves more than the usual amount of corruption. The peaceful transfer of power is likely to continue.

The Costa Rican Constitution was adopted after a disputed election in 1948 that produced the bloodiest war in the country's history. That document tried to eliminate everything that would lead the country away from the peaceful way of life the locals favor. It eliminated the military and set election rules to try to account for every possible contingency.

There is even a rule that covers what will occur in the event of an exact tie. I was gratified to learn that should such an incredible long shot come up, the oldest candidate will be declared the winner. In this case Oscar Arias, the former president and Nobel Peace Prize winner. Geezers everywhere can take heart. There is a beautiful, peaceful country in Central America that loves us.

The Prince of Produce

The sign reads *Super Mercado*, meaning 'super market' but the word *super* lends a grandeur to the establishment that exists only in the mind of its owner. The whole store would fit into the snack food section of a typical Winn Dixie. I was doing my first tour of the biggest super market in our little *barrio* in Heredia, Costa Rica. I will be doing a lot of shopping there in the next year or so.

The layout of the place was vaguely familiar. Only the shotgun toting guard in the bullet proof vest at the door caught me by surprise. Rows of shelves are stocked with packages. Glass front freezers and coolers line the back wall. A long glass cooler displays fresh meat and fish. The meat isn't wrapped in neat packages. Bins in the cooler overflow with chicken, fish, pork and beef. The bins are sorted by animal and body part, priced in *colones* per kilogram, large numbers representing small money.

The meat looked fresh. Four butchers worked the busy counter. I struggled to remember the Spanish word for five hundred; *gramos* was easy. I gave up and ordered six hundred grams of chicken, 600 being one of the few numbers larger than 10 that I know in Spanish.

I toured aisles stacked with products I will probably never try including loaves of bread hard as bricks, lots of cookies and sweets, and enough canned goods and dried beans to pull the country through a nuclear winter. Then I noticed the little side-room produce section. It was about the size of a large tool shed.

Fruit and vegetables covered three walls. The table in the center left just enough room to walk around it. The table featured tropical favorites, papayas as big as footballs, pineapples even bigger, guavas, and oranges. But what caught my eye was a display on the right-hand wall dedicated to the Prince of Produce, the King of Crops, the Hermaphrodite of the Harvest, the noble tomato.

Ever since childhood summers on my grandma's stoop with a tomato in one hand and a salt shaker in the other, I've had a fervent attachment to the pulpy red fruit.

For many years I'd resigned myself to the disappearance of the delicious vine ripened tomatoes of my youth. To one used to the pale shrink-wrapped, ethylene-gassed fare of my homeland, the pile of firm, ripe orbs on display here in Santa Barbara looked like a shrine. Every specimen showed the deep yellow-red, the plump, mature firmness and the classic, sunken, Buddha's belly-button stem scars of the truly fine eating tomato.

Without having given it a thought I had stumbled into the native land of this wonderful treat, *solanum lycopersicum*. Cultivated by Central America's native Mayans, the tomato is a member of the nightshade family, which includes eggplant, spuds, and a number of uniquely poisonous plants like belladonna. It features history and legend as flavorful and appealing as a good pizza.

The tomato is scientifically a fruit although served and used as a vegetable. The term "vegetable" has no scientific definition. Always ready to make the language fit Uncle Sam's need for revenue, the U.S. Supreme Court ruled the tomato a vegetable for tax purposes in Nix v. Hedden in 1893. Fruit was exempt from tax.

Because of its close relations in the nightshade family, most Colonial Americans believed tomatoes were poisonous. Thomas Jefferson is among those enlightened souls who knew better, cultivating them at Monticello. The Puritans shunned the red orbs for their reputed effect as a powerful aphrodisiac. I live in hope and lay on the ketchup.

Legend has it that the matter of the wholesomeness of tomatoes was put to rest in 1820, when Colonel Robert Gibbon Johnson announced that at noon on September 26, he would eat a basket of tomatoes in front of the Salem, New Jersey courthouse. A crowd of some 2,000 is reported to have gathered to witness Johnson's death. They were shocked, and likely disappointed, when he survived.

By the 1830s the tomato had gone from poison to wonder drug. There followed a tomato craze of sorts. Tomatoes were said to cure diseases from dysentery to cholera. You could buy tomato pills at the local pharmacy. It is doubtful that tomatoes cured any diseases. It is not too far fetched, however, to think that eating tomatoes could have had a salutary effect on patients who had given up such popular remedies as mercury and bleeding.

By the time the tomato mania ended, the bright red fruit was an established part of the American diet. I'm delighted to find they are even more of a staple of the Central American diet.

I was ready to pay any price, but when I finally did the math to see what this precious commodity was worth, I had to do it twice in blinking disbelief. The sign said *C* 220/*kg* (220 *colones/kilo*). That's 20 cents a pound in dollars. I resisted buying the whole pile, but only just. If God eats, He eats tomatoes like these every single day. And I'll bet He eats them on fresh baked corn tortillas if He can find them.

Nurturing Cultural Intercourse and English Language Dignity

*WARNING: PG13 RATED ESSAY, MAY NOT BE
SUITABLE FOR YOUNG CHILDREN
OR PRUDISH BUSYBODIES.*

The school is a single room concrete block building up in the hills behind Santa Ana in Costa Rica. It's poorly lit and cheaply furnished in the Costa Rican style. I spend four hours a week there teaching a few of the locals how to speak English. My students range in age from 14 to 64. A group of about half a dozen forms the dedicated core of our student body, another half a dozen drift in and out, attending classes sporadically.

Some evenings, especially now in the rainy season, there are only two or three students in class. They get a lot more practice in the smaller classes and improvement is often noticeable in a single lesson. Progress is gratifying for them and for me.

I've been teaching there for over six months now. We've become comfortable with one another. The classes are relaxed and fun. My ability as an expert speaker of English and determined, if often unintentionally amusing, speaker of Spanish seem to be appreciated.

We were nearing the end of a class in which there were only two students, both attractive, married Costa Rican women in their twenties. Both have been in my class since I began teaching. I sometimes give one of them a ride to the nearest bus stop after class, but tonight she didn't need it. She explained, "Dees night I going sleep wid my moother."

I explained that it would probably sound better to say, "I am going to stay with my mother" because of the other meaning of "sleep with" in English. She understood immediately and both women were delighted to have picked up this titillating scrap of English. Apparently I'd touched on a topic here that both women had been harboring some curiosity about.

They wanted to know if they could ask me something without embarrassing me. I told them it was hard to embarrass me in Spanish, because I'm too busy translating in my head for embarrassment and the entire language sounds like it came out of a medical textbook.

At least that's what I think I told them.

Whatever I told them, they immediately wanted to know how to say things in English that most definitely could embarrass me in my native language. We worked through a few Spanish expressions I'd never heard before. The translations weren't too bad until we reached *chupa el pene*. They wanted to know what that was in English. They had to say it a couple times, because I'd never heard the Spanish verb *chupar* before. They finally snapped on the lights in the thick *gringo* skull with a delicate Spanish description of fellatio: *besos intimos* or intimate kisses.

They had no problem being embarrassed in Spanish. But their curiosity and eagerness to know some real hot English allowed them to persevere.

They were visibly disappointed when I told them it's almost the same as the Spanish, *felación*. They knew there was more than that. One of them said to me in Spanish, "My doctor would call it that. What do the regular people (*gente corriente*) call it?"

My students know that English is thick with the kind of snappy expressions they hear in pop music all the time. The hard-hitting Anglo-Saxon words, unavailable in their Latinate native tongue, give English a unique punch and power.

The prospect of telling these women that we refer to fellatio as a "blow job," however, was more revealing of the raw, vulgar side of English than I wanted to be. And the other Anglo-Saxon possibilities for verb and object were equally crude. Sure, they were punchy. And the girls would have been happy to know them. But there is such a thing as too punchy, too raw, too commercial somehow for a first exposure to the erotic side of English. Or maybe I'm just too much of a romantic, crusty old fart to teach street English to Costa Rican housewives.

Whatever the reason, I felt like I'd be doing grave harm to Latin American relations and insulting the rich legacy of such English language luminaries as Shakespeare, Frost, Coleridge, and Dickenson if I taught these two charming women the term "blow job." And besides, I didn't know the Spanish word for "blow" which I knew I was going to have to translate.

But neither did I want to disappoint them. I have my reputation as an expert *profesor de inglés* to maintain. Thinking back to their blushing descriptions of the besos intimos, I decided on "kiss the pickle." Cheerful, friendly, almost cute. They looked puzzled at first, probably baffled by "pickle." I translated helpfully, *"Besar el pepino."* What a hit. It was the funniest thing they'd heard since the last time I tried to say *espectacularísimamente*. They were thrilled.

We spent the best five minutes of my English teaching career trying to work the Spanish accent out of "kees da peekehl." Working through common expressions using "kiss the pickle" was the kind of language learning exercise you just don't get with Berlitz courses. It was way more fun than my previous favorites "pretty tasty" and "skewered shrimp" had ever been. I came away gratified at my success in both advancing intercultural under-standing and preserving a measure of genial dignity for the English language.

At least, that's what I think I did.

Made in the USA
Las Vegas, NV
12 November 2021